MORE
VEGGIES
PLEASE!

5 cups
of spinach

MORE VEGGIES PLEASE!

Easy Kid-Approved Meals and Family-Friendly Comfort Foods with Surprising Veggie Twists

NIKKI DINKI

BenBella Books, Inc.
Dallas, TX

BenBella Books, Inc.
10440 N. Central Expressway
Suite 800
Dallas, TX 75231
www.benbellabooks.com
Send feedback to feedback@benbellabooks.com

BenBella is a federally registered trademark

Printed in the United States of America
10 9 8 7 6 5 4 3 2 1

Library of Congress Control Number: 2021006211
ISBN 9781953295569
eISBN 9781953295903

Food photography by Andreana Bitsis; food
    styling by Tracy Carter (head stylist), Missy
    Fernandez (assistant stylist), and Stefanie Baum
    (cover stylist)
Lifestyle/family photos on pages 2, 19, 35, and 133
    by Barbara Brady; on page 249 courtesy of the
    author; all others by David Nicholas Photography
Editing by Tami Root Frocchi and Claire Schulz
Copyediting by Jennifer Greenstein

Proofreading by Lisa Story and Karen Wise
Indexing by WordCo Indexing Services, Inc.
Text design by Kit Sweeney
Cover design by Brigid Pearson and
    Heather Butterfield
Cover photography by
    David Nicholas Photography
Printed by Versa Press

Special discounts for bulk sales are available. Please
contact **bulkorders@benbellabooks.com**.

FOR IVY, OWEN, DAISY + WILLA,
WHO HOLD MY HEART
IN THEIR LITTLE HANDS

CONTENTS

more veggies on the side and at snack time

veggies . . . for dessert!

Zucchini Biscuits
(page 39)

Sweet Potato
Cinnamon Rolls
(page 219)

Cauliflower Chive
Risotto (page 134)

INTRO

I *love* veggies, but getting my kids to love them is a work in progress. I guess this shouldn't come as a surprise considering I didn't willingly eat my first vegetable until the age of 20—the name "Picky Nikki" still follows me to this day. And although my kids are good eaters (better than I ever was!), they aren't great ones, so getting them to eat more vegetables is one of my top priorities.

I always include delicious veggies on their plates, but I don't stress when those veggies go untouched (which happens . . . often). That's because my cooking incorporates vegetables at every turn. The kids may not have eaten their peas at dinner, but they enjoyed cauliflower and sweet potatoes in their mac and cheese, devoured spinach eggs at breakfast, and asked for more eggplant chicken tenders at lunch!

What I've learned—and what might surprise you—is that veggies aren't just good for our bodies; they also have the potential to enhance the flavor, texture, and overall deliciousness of our favorite dishes. For instance, the finely chopped mushrooms in my burgers intensify the beefy flavor while melting into the patty, and the roasted eggplant I use to replace eggs for breading chicken keeps the chicken irresistibly moist while adding the most delightful touch of smokiness (get ready for some *insanely* delicious chicken Parm). And yes, it's pretty fun—and 100 percent satisfying—to watch my kids eat mushrooms and eggplant in these ways when they would never touch them otherwise.

What's really great is that cooking this way requires no fancy ingredients or complicated cooking techniques—hey, sometimes I don't even have time for a shower; I can't be spending hours on dinner! These are easy, accessible recipes that have been tested hundreds of times, by both me and other parents, to ensure that they work—every time, in every kitchen—perfectly. This book is a collection of my most tried-and-true dishes, ones that wow both picky eaters and foodie parents alike. The recipes here are simply the *best* mashed potatoes, chicken tenders, and penne alla vodka you will ever have—and they also just so happen to be jam-packed with high-protein beans and nutrient-rich vegetables. Soon you'll be sitting back with a full belly at a quiet table, vaguely remembering that, oh yeah, your super satisfying, dinner party–worthy meal also contained veggies. TONS. OF. VEGGIES!

ABOUT ME, "PICKY NIKKI" DINKI

I grew up right smack in the middle of a big family of five kids. Life was delightfully loud and there was always someone running around the house,

I ate my first veggie at 20 years old

usually hitting up "the loop"—through the kitchen, down the hallway, around that hairpin turn in the foyer, over the cat, past the living room couches, and back into the kitchen, grabbing a handful of Lucky Charms for the victory lap. *Whew!*

In all that chaos, it probably wasn't hard to miss the little girl sneaking away from the dinner table to throw her veggies down the open air vent (I didn't confess until the smell became unbearable). I gave my parents a run for their money; I was a picky eater from day one, and I was stubborn as all hell. If my mom said I couldn't leave the table until I ate my dinner, I simply didn't leave—I sat there like a statue until she gave up and sent me to bed. If my parents forced me to try something new, I would act like a person with a spider in her pants, jumping, screaming, and rolling on the floor as soon as it touched my lips. So when I was 10 years old, they threw in the towel; I was allowed to eat whatever

I obviously love cooking with veggies, but I also love growing them!

I wanted, but my mom was not going to make me a separate meal—I would have to cook for myself.

Well! This preteen chef whipped up a dizzying array of meals, including ramen noodles, mac and cheese, and cereal, all in constant rotation. As a kid, I was happy as a clam with this diet plan, but as an adult, I discovered that my body couldn't take the lack of nutrition any longer. I wasn't getting what I needed to keep up with long nights bartending and early mornings pursuing the arts in NYC. And it was downright embarrassing ordering off the kids' menu on first dates. It was time to change, and that was scary.

At 20 years old, I still *hated* veggies—with one exception: I had started eating jarred marinara sauce over pasta (only one particular brand, of course). So when considering giving veggies a shot, I thought that since my taste buds were actually okay with this jarred sauce, eating a raw tomato couldn't be *that* far off, right? I took a baby step and cooked *actual tomatoes*, adding them to the "Picky Nikki"–approved store-bought marinara sauce. It was different, but not *too* different, and I got used to it. From there, I started making my own simple three-ingredient sauce and slowly learned to like that as well. Through a long process of cooking the tomatoes less and less, I actually got to a point where I could say—with a straight face—that I liked, and possibly even, gulp, *loved* tomatoes.

So then I thought, *If I could go from hating tomatoes to loving them, what else could I add to my list?*

I tried more vegetables, and tried and tried, and cooked and cooked. It was years in the making, but the love affair blossomed and I found my veggie soul mates. And my cooking grew too! This new love of eating and cooking was a beautiful whirlwind that took over my other creative pursuits and became the focus of my home and work life. I felt like I was finally on the right path, and who could have ever imagined it would be a path paved with veggies?

I tell you all of this because if your kids (or you!) are on the picky side, I come to you from a place of understanding. I've been there. And although I'm all about the veggies now, Picky Nikki is still somewhere inside me. I empathize with her and listen to her when making and testing these recipes. I don't want to push the flavors too far, but I *am* giving a little nudge to create dishes that not only are more nutritious but are the ultimate versions of everything we love.

MORE NUTRITIOUS COOKING!

Some people will flip through this cookbook and be appalled to see ingredients like butter, sugar, and white flour. "I thought this was a healthy cookbook!" they will say. Well, that depends on your definition of healthy. To me, the version of healthy you'll find in this book can be summed up as "more nutritious cooking." Take my flagship mac and cheese recipe, for instance; it's definitely more nutritious than your average mac—there are 6 cups of veggies in it! But in that comfort-food classic, the mac is no good without the cheese, so you can be sure there's plenty of that too.

This way of thinking all started when I found myself asking similar questions over and over:

- When we make a "healthy" version of something, why does it have to be SO healthy?

- Why does a dish have to go from 500 calories to 50?

- Why does a cauliflower Alfredo sauce have to be made with only pureed cauliflower? (Gross! What happened to the butter and Parm?)

- Why can't we find the middle ground—and make something that ups the nutritional ante but still tastes great and stays true to the original?

And because I couldn't find the answers, I decided to redefine "healthy" myself. Don't get me wrong, I'm not saying that I can't make you an ultra-flavorful, low-cal, low-carb meal that will knock your socks off. But what I *am* saying is that I can't make you mac and cheese without actual *cheese* or brownies without sugar—at least, not if you want to love them as much as your grandma's.

So, this *is* a healthy cookbook—in a way that's a little old-school and a little new-school. I don't want to revamp your family's whole diet, but I do want to give you *incredibly delicious*, easy options for cooking with and eating more and more veggies. Wholesome, homemade meals with tons of veggies—this is definitely healthy cooking to me.

NOT A REPLACEMENT FOR A SIDE OF VEGGIES

That said, these recipes are not replacements for whole vegetables. I still give my kids raw and cooked whole veggies like broccoli, sweet potatoes, and carrots at every meal. I watch as they slowly get used to the unadulterated flavors and textures of those veggies, and I stick to it, putting them on their plates again and again (and I try not to get discouraged when it's me who ends up eating them again and again). Eventually, though, they pick up those veggies, taste them, eat them, and even—over time—learn to love them. This approach is working for us, and it might just work for you.

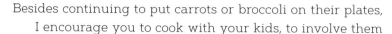

Besides continuing to put carrots or broccoli on their plates, I encourage you to cook with your kids, to involve them in the process of incorporating those veggies into their foods. My kids help me measure the cups of spinach that make up their favorite Double Chocolate Chip Muffins, and they love squishing the peas for their weekly requested Pea Guacamole. They may not taste those ingredients strongly in the finished products, but they will start to think positively about them and will be more inclined to give those veggies a shot in their whole form one day.

My eating journey took me from hating vegetables to loving them, so I know from experience that the more my kids eat veggies, the more they'll like them. Those whole veggies on their plates along with the more subtle ones swimming throughout my recipes are all great steps in the right direction. And even if you are as veggie averse as your kids, I promise you can do this! Honestly, if "Picky Nikki" can do it, anyone can.

ABOUT THE RECIPES

These days, I have a lot of professional titles—Chef, Author, TV Host, Most Animated (and Slightly Ridiculous) Bedtime Story Reader—but the title I hold in highest regard is that of Recipe Developer. That might seem obvious since you're reading a book of my personally developed recipes. But a true recipe developer is someone who goes beyond jotting down a recipe they just made for dinner. My recipes go through an intense process. There's brainstorming, writing, testing, testing, testing, testing, crowd-sourced testing, more brainstorming, and more testing, and finally the polished version comes to you. I want to anticipate your problems, give you the substitutions when I know you'll need them, and figure out what pitfalls or questions might pop up as you go along. And then, of course, I want more than just *my* family to agree that each recipe is absolutely, undeniably, ridiculously delicious!

EASY + THOUGHTFUL

One reason I test so thoroughly is that I'm making a constant effort to streamline my recipes. If I think I can shave 10 minutes off your cook time, I'm going to do it (that's 10 minutes you could use to shake a cocktail, text that school mom back, *and* post about your awesomeness on Instagram). And if the traditional version of a recipe always calls for egg whites—or worse, eggs at room temperature (who ever remembers to do that?)—you know I'm going to test to see whether those scary, whole, straight-from-the-fridge eggs really are a deal-breaker. (Spoiler alert! They rarely are.)

I also consider the best tools for the job. I try the recipes in every appliance and pan I can find to give you options for using what's most convenient for *you*. And after all that testing, I'll let you know when that cast-iron pan or food processor actually *is* vital to the final outcome.

I GOT YOUR BACK

I want you to feel like I've always got your back—because I do. The batter looks too thick? *Eh, no worries—Nikki said right here that it might "look as thick as pizza dough."* Cookies not forming? *Oh, it's okay, Nikki said if that happens, I should add more flour.*

My biggest fear is that you'll feel lost halfway through a recipe or invest your precious time and have a total mess of a dish in the end. I know everyone tells you how easy cooking is, and it can be, but there *is* a lot to learn. The good news is that I have squeezed every word I could into this book to help you with anything and everything that might come up. And when you are looking for a short cut, **Hack It** is here with ways to veggie-fy store-bought ingredients. And **Freeze It** is here to help with all your make-ahead and meal prep plans. Take this journey with me—know that you *can* make pierogies, homemade pasta, and your own jam—and I am here to help.

A WORD ON THE INGREDIENTS

When it comes to ingredients, I take a hard look at what makes an impact on a recipe's outcome and what can be cut. And I'm always striving to make shopping easy and to leave you with minimal waste or "extra" ingredients (I want you to be able to use up that entire can of pumpkin once you've opened it). And if I can't find a way to use something up, you better believe I'll offer you clever ways to store it and use it in other recipes.

I also want you to be able to shop for these recipes anywhere. There will be no need to hunt around at gourmet shops for yucca or truffled Brie. In this book, you will find only two ingredients I consider "specialty"—wheat germ and chia seeds (see What You Need to Know on page 9). And although they might be a little special, they're both becoming widely available, and you'll find

that they last forever. But that's not to say they're going to sit in your pantry—I use them in tons of recipes throughout the book (always giving substitutions if they're just not your thing). Soon you'll learn just how they can transform your cooking by adding serious nutritional punches and very little extra effort.

All in all, these thoughtful little features add up to make my recipes as fast and easy as possible. You should be spending more time around the table eating and enjoying with family and friends than sweating in the kitchen.

CLASSIC, REMIX + TOP 10

Not sure where to start your veggie journey? Well, there are three different designations in this book meant to guide you on your way: Classic, Remix, and the revered Top Ten.

 Looking for the most old-school version of a recipe—something like traditional, buttery biscuits? Just keep your eye out for the recipes with the Classic flag. You'll get those same flavors and textures you're used to, and although there will always be a veggie twist (hello, there's zucchini in your biscuits!), it will be a more subtle one.

 Then, when you're ready to take it up a notch, Remix is there for you. These recipe versions are inspired by the classics but take things a step further in terms of the veggie twists. For instance, the Remix of those buttery biscuits mentioned above are my Carrot Biscuits—inviting you in with a vibrant orange sunrise color and crunchy cinnamon–brown sugar topping.

 And when you are simply looking for a "wow!" recipe jam-packed with veggies and sure to become your new favorite masterpiece to bring to a party, check out the Top Ten. These were voted on by hundreds of people and are a great place to start your veggie adventure.

RECIPE CHECKLIST

When I love a cookbook, I find it helpful to check off the recipes I've made, make notes about the dish, and even give ratings so I remember all my favorites. So, on page 250 you'll find a Recipe Checklist where you can do all these things that much more easily. And if you want to be a **More Veggies Please MVP!**, see if you can make them all!

WHAT YOU NEED TO KNOW

Because I want to set you up for success, here are answers to some of my recipe testers' FAQs. I'm also including more details on ingredients and tips to make your veggie-focused cooking as streamlined as possible.

SPECIALTY INGREDIENTS

As mentioned, I call for only two "weird" ingredients—chia seeds and wheat germ—and I call for them for a reason.

CHIA SEEDS: Chia seeds have the unique ability to absorb water and thicken things. Using chia seeds allows you to create awesome textures like those of my Strawberry + Chia Jam (page 90) and Strawberry Cheesecake Chia Seed Pudding (page 34). Chia seeds also deliver immense amounts of protein, fiber, antioxidants, and calcium. They're serious little powerhouses! Another point in their favor is that you can find them almost anywhere you buy groceries.

WHEAT GERM: Wheat germ is also easy to find (it's probably in your store, although you may never have looked for it—check the cereal aisle). It's basically flavorless (if anything, it's got a pleasant slight nuttiness), and its coarse but delicate texture allows it to be easily incorporated into tons of dishes.

chia seeds

Daisy, AKA Garden Tomato Thief

Wheat germ is the heart of the wheat kernel, and it's the part richest in vitamins, minerals, protein, and fiber.

So that's why I wanted to throw a couple of unique ingredients your way. They're used in multiple recipes throughout this book, so if you buy them, they will not go to waste. *However*, if there are no chia seeds or wheat germ in your pantry, have no fear. I will always offer you substitutions for these ingredients in any recipes that call for them.

GENERAL NOTES

FAT CONTENT: If I don't specify the fat content of the milk or the fat ratio of the beef, it's because it doesn't matter; the recipe is flexible and you can use whatever you have on hand. That said, in my own kitchen I do generally cook with full-fat milk, yogurt, and sour cream, and I use an 80/20 blend for my beef.

OIL: I use olive oil as my main cooking oil for sautéing, but you can use whatever oil you like with no big flavor difference. And in recipes where I call for neutral oils for baking or frying, I specify canola or avocado, as those are the best and most accessible in my opinion. However, other oils like vegetable oil, grapeseed oil, and corn oil do work.

WATER IS YOUR BEST FRIEND: I find the biggest tip to ensure properly creamy dishes and incredible leftovers is . . . water! So simple. A splash of water can save your Alfredo if it thickened too much on the stove, and a little water can make leftover mac and cheese taste like you just made it fresh. So don't be afraid of some H_2O; if you add too much, just cook for an extra minute until it evaporates.

SALT: I call for kosher salt in this book and tested all these recipes with Morton brand salt, as I have found it is the

most commonly used brand in home cooking. In comparison to brands like Diamond Crystal, Morton is much saltier. (If you use Diamond Crystal, you will generally need to add additional salt to the measurements I give.) I always encourage tasting your food as often as possible while you're cooking. It's the only way to truly add the correct amount of salt. My amounts are a good place to start, but with varying factors like the saltiness of different stocks and cheeses, only you can properly salt your dish.

WEIGHT MEASUREMENTS: When you see an ingredient listed like this zucchini from my Zucchini Biscuits: *1 medium zucchini (7 ounces), peeled + coarsely chopped (1½ cups),* the ounce amount always refers to the whole, unpeeled zucchini. The ounce amount is there to help you know what to buy at the store. Once it is peeled and chopped, it will be less than 7 ounces.

VEGGIE NOTES

EGGPLANT PUREE: All the recipes in this book that use eggplant call for 1 medium eggplant to be pureed, which should yield 1 cup. So when baking up the eggplant for a recipe, feel free to bake extra, puree it all, and then freeze in 1-cup portions— the perfect amount for all of my eggplant-based recipes, like my favorite, Eggplant Chicken Tenders (page 82), and Eggplant Parm Meatballs (page 128).

CAULIFLOWER RICE: I call for a lot of cauliflower rice in this book, as it's an easy, prechopped ingredient found almost anywhere. My recipes use fresh or frozen cauliflower rice interchangeably, and I'll always mention whether it's necessary to thaw your frozen cauliflower rice (it rarely is). If you can't get your hands on the store-bought stuff, you can easily make cauliflower rice at home; just pulse cauliflower florets in your food processor until you get very finely chopped pieces that look like rice. I sometimes actually prefer the homemade version, as the store-bought can occasionally be on the coarsely chopped side, but all kinds work for my recipes.

POTATOES: I often suggest cooking potatoes and sweet potatoes in the microwave because this saves a huge amount of time. However, any time I call for cooking potatoes in the microwave, you can always cook them in the oven instead. Just poke holes in the potato and bake at 425°F for 50 to 60 minutes, until very tender. You can also look for canned sweet potato puree. It's a great time saver for recipes like my Sweet Potato Tortillas (page 88) or my Sweet Potato Cinnamon Rolls (page 219).

OATS: Many people use different types of oats interchangeably. While this may work for your oatmeal, my recipes call for certain types of oats for a reason. For example, if I call for quick oats, it's because they are more broken down than old-fashioned oats, and in recipes like my granola bars this allows them to form better. So be on the lookout for what kind of oats I call for, and try to stick to them.

BEANS: There are also lots of beans in this book! I love that beans are easy to find, cheap to buy, and packaged conveniently in long-lasting cans. I call for cannellini beans in most of my recipes, but you can swap them out for other white beans such as great northern or navy (pinto beans, chickpeas, and black beans are generally *not* good swaps for cannellini). *Note:* One 15-ounce can beans = 1½ cups cooked beans.

BUTTERNUT SQUASH: I love frozen butternut squash; it's precooked, prechopped, and perfect for my recipes. *But* you can also use fresh squash in any of these recipes. Just cut your squash small and be sure to steam or simmer it first so it's tender.

BEETS: I often use precooked beets (found in the produce section) or canned beets—because I'm lazy like that. However, if you prefer to

roast fresh beets, cut off their stems, then wrap them whole and unpeeled in foil. Bake at 400°F until they can be pierced easily with a knife—45 to 60 minutes. Use a paper towel to rub off the skins, then use as directed in the recipe.

SPINACH: With just a few exceptions, I tend to use fresh baby spinach in my recipes. It's usually sold prewashed and it doesn't need to be thawed. Though with a deft hand you could sub regular or frozen spinach for baby spinach in my recipes, that changes the ratios and the amount of liquid would need to be adjusted for each particular dish. It's a little tricky! So I suggest sticking to baby spinach in the recipes that call for it.

So that's What You Need to Know. And don't worry: there are plenty more helpful explanations, tips, and tricks in every recipe.

MORE VEGGIES AT BREAKFAST

It's always carbs, sugar, and maybe some protein, but vegetables are not usually invited to the breakfast party. Well, it's time to rewrite the invitations! I've got bagels with cauliflower, pancakes with beans, and even French toast with zucchini. These veggies are all seamlessly integrated to give breakfast a much-needed boost—while still satisfying those morning cravings your blood sugar is begging for. Believe me, Lucky Charms will always have a special place in my heart, but these breakfast foods will actually feed your heart.

cauliflower + yogurt bagels

One day my daughter came home from a cooking class at school with a two-ingredient bagel (yogurt + self-rising flour)—and it was *so* good! I immediately started thinking about what veggies I could throw at it. Cauliflower rice was the winner as it required no extra prep, it was subtle in flavor and color, and the dough could be made by hand (although the food processor is a bit faster and makes for an extra-smooth dough). In the end I got perfect little bagels, ready for whatever toppings you like. Consider sprinkling with sesame or poppy seeds, or making my cinnamon raisin version—there really is something for everyone.

— MAKES 8 MINI BAGELS —

2 cups all-purpose flour + more as needed

1½ teaspoons baking powder

1 teaspoon kosher salt

1 cup plain Greek yogurt (8 ounces; see note)

1 cup **cauliflower rice**, fresh or thawed from frozen (3 ounces; see note)

TOPPING

1 large egg

Everything Bagel Seasoning (page 20), poppy seeds, or sesame seeds (optional)

CINNAMON RAISIN VERSION

In Step 1, add 2 tablespoons brown sugar and 2 teaspoons ground cinnamon to the flour mixture. Once the dough has come together, place ½ cup raisins on your counter and put the dough on top of the raisins. Knead the dough a couple of times until the raisins are fully incorporated. Continue on with Step 2.

1 Preheat the oven to 350°F. Prepare a baking sheet with parchment or cooking oil spray.

BY HAND: Mix the flour, baking powder, and salt in a large bowl. Then add the yogurt and cauliflower rice (your rice should be raw at this point, or thawed from frozen) and continue to mix well until the ingredients blend into a dough.

FOOD PROCESSOR OR STAND MIXER: The food processor is my favorite method, as it breaks down any large chunks of cauliflower, resulting in an extra-smooth dough (the stand mixer doesn't make the dough any smoother, but does make the process very quick). Simply process all the ingredients in the food processor (or combine in a mixer) until a dough forms (it's okay if it's a little crumbly as long as it sticks together nicely when squeezed). Note that when your dough has formed, it's okay if it's a little tacky, but it shouldn't be so sticky that it attaches to your hands. If you find this is the case, add extra flour, ¼ cup at a time, until you reach a workable consistency.

2 On a lightly floured surface, form the dough into a ball and divide the dough equally into eight pieces; I like to do this by cutting the round of dough in half, then cutting each of the halves into four pieces, like how you cut a pizza. Form the dough pieces into balls, then flatten them slightly and create the bagel holes by pushing your finger into the center of each piece of dough. Transfer the bagels to the prepared baking sheet.

3 Whisk the egg and 1 tablespoon water together in a small bowl, then brush this mixture over the tops of the bagels. Next—become your own bagel shop!—top the bagels with

CONTINUED . . .

step 1

step 2

. . . CONTINUED

your choice of Everything Bagel Seasoning (page 20), poppy seeds, or sesame seeds, or just leave them plain. If you decide not to use seasoning, you should still brush them with the egg as it makes for a perfectly golden-brown bagel.

4 Bake the bagels until they are lightly golden brown—30 to 35 minutes. Let them cool before eating and enjoy with cream cheese, butter, or my Strawberry + Chia Jam (page 90).

NOTES
For this recipe, 1½ cups cauliflower florets should give you the cup of cauliflower rice needed.
I generally use full-fat yogurt, but any fat content will work here.

STORE IT + FREEZE IT
To store, place bagels in an airtight container and store on the counter for up to 5 days. To freeze, freeze the completely cooled bagels in an airtight container for up to 5 months. To thaw, bake at 350°F for 12 to 15 minutes or microwave on high for 30 seconds. I also like to slice my cooled bagels in half before freezing so that I can pop a presliced frozen bagel directly into the toaster oven to thaw and toast at the same time.

avocado + pea toast

I love avocados, I love tomatoes, I love everything bagels, but I do *not* love—or even like—peas. Wait, let me be clear—sugar snap peas, snow peas, now *they* are delicious. But your standard frozen peas are not my friends, and my kids have followed in my footsteps in also declaring them untouchable. So why is it that I keep them on hand? Well, I'll let you in on a little secret: they blend in seamlessly with avocados. And when I top this avocado and pea combo with quick-but-flavorful fixin's like Everything Bagel Seasoning, I'm suddenly eating peas left and right—and so are the kids. So keep the peas comin'!

MAKES 2 SLICES OF TOAST

1 large **avocado** (10 ounces)

Juice of 1 lemon (2 tablespoons)

¼ cup frozen **peas** (1 ounce), thawed

Kosher salt

2 large slices whole-grain bread, toasted

1 teaspoon + 1 teaspoon Everything Bagel Seasoning (recipe below), divided

½ medium **tomato** (4 ounces), cut into 4 slices

½ teaspoon olive oil

1 Cut the avocado in half, remove the pit, cut off ½ inch from each end, and peel off the skin (cutting off the ends should make it easy for you to peel the skin off in one piece). Put half of the avocado in a medium bowl and slice the other half into ¼-inch-thick slices (you should end up with 8 to 10 slices). Sprinkle each half with lemon juice.

2 Add the peas and a large pinch of salt to the avocado in the bowl. Using a fork, mash the avocado, peas, and salt until the ingredients are well combined and mostly smooth. Alternatively, for a super smooth spread, you can blend the avocado mixture in a food processor.

3 Spread the avocado-pea mixture onto each slice of toasted bread. Layer the sliced avocado on top of the avocado spread, then sprinkle with 1 teaspoon of the Everything Bagel Seasoning. Layer the tomato slices on top of the avocado, drizzle with the olive oil, then finish off by sprinkling with the remaining 1 teaspoon Everything Bagel Seasoning. Serve immediately.

everything bagel seasoning

MAKES 2½ TEASPOONS

½ teaspoon kosher salt

½ teaspoon poppy seeds

½ teaspoon sesame seeds

½ teaspoon dried minced garlic

½ teaspoon dried minced onion

Combine the salt, poppy seeds, sesame seeds, minced garlic, and minced onion in a small bowl and stir to combine.

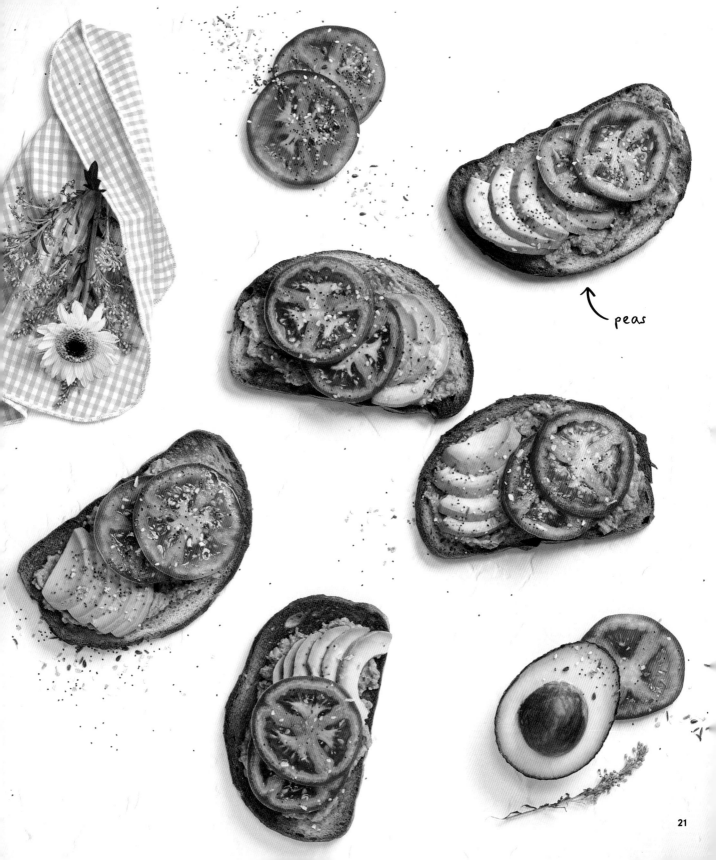

peas

21

cauliflower scrambled eggs

As much as I love adding veggies to dishes, I hate adding cooking time or overcomplicating recipes, especially when they are super simple to begin with—like scrambled eggs. So for these eggs, I'm adding the veggies as quickly and easily as possible. Cauliflower rice can be bought premade fresh or frozen, eliminating prep time. Its super small size also allows it to cook up in a flash, and its mild taste and color don't overwhelm the eggs. I don't know about you, but cauliflower isn't often served up next to the eggs and bacon in my house, so even just a little cauliflower at breakfast is a big win.

SERVES 1

2 large eggs
Kosher salt
1 teaspoon unsalted butter
2 tablespoons **cauliflower rice**, fresh or frozen

1 In a small bowl, whisk together the eggs and a pinch of salt. Heat the butter in a small nonstick skillet over medium heat, then add the cauliflower rice (no need to thaw if frozen) and another pinch of salt. Sauté until the cauliflower rice is very soft—3 to 4 minutes.

2 Add the eggs to the pan and continue cooking, stirring constantly until the eggs are moist but not runny—about 2 minutes. Serve hot.

SERVING SUGGESTIONS

Try these with White Bean Pancakes + Waffles (page 25) or Cauliflower + Yogurt Bagels (page 17). Or use in a breakfast quesadilla or egg sandwich Yum!

NOTE

In a pinch for a pinch of cauliflower rice? Use a box grater or Microplane with medium-sized holes to grate a couple of cauliflower florets directly into the pan.

EVEN MORE VEGGIES!

Although the ratio of 2 tablespoons cauliflower to 2 eggs isn't a ton, it's as much as you can get away with without detecting any cauliflower taste. However, add some cheese to mask the flavor and you can double the amount of cauliflower.

cheesy green eggs

top ten

remix

Green is gorgeous! Start with a handful of baby spinach along with some eggs and cheese in a blender and end with beautifully fluffy eggs. Though the veggie is more noticeable here (hello, green!), these scrambled eggs were a huge favorite among my extensive group of taste testers (hello, Top Ten!). Even more importantly, most kids, surprisingly, weren't bothered by the green color and instead found it a fun change. Sounds like your breakfast might be looking a bit greener from now on.

——————————— SERVES 1 ———————————

½ cup **baby spinach** (½ ounce)

2 large eggs

¼ cup shredded mozzarella cheese

Kosher salt

1 teaspoon unsalted butter

1 Blend the spinach, eggs, mozzarella, and a pinch of salt in a blender (or food processor) on high until the spinach leaves are fully pureed.

2 Heat the butter in a small nonstick skillet over medium heat, then transfer the spinach mixture to the skillet. Cook the mixture, stirring constantly, until the eggs are moist but not runny— about 4 minutes. Serve hot.

SERVING SUGGESTION

Serve these green eggs with Carrot Biscuits (page 43) for a truly colorful breakfast.

white bean pancakes + waffles

"Is that a box of *store-bought* pancake/waffle mix in the ingredients? I thought this was a reputable cookbook!" said no one ever—because the majority of us use the store-bought stuff and love it. I tested this recipe *a lot* (good thing my kids never say no to pancakes), and no matter how many times I made my own mixes, the versions tested with store-bought mix were always better. Most store-bought mixes include extra ingredients that help pancakes and waffles rise and give them structure, which really allows the beans and pancake mix to marry beautifully.

So without further ado, I present the most incredible pancakes, complete with a can of beans! And if you throw this mix in the waffle iron, you are in for a real treat, perfectly crisp and slightly moist in the middle. They have become my Sunday morning staple.

—————————————— MAKES 10 PANCAKES OR 8 WAFFLES ——————————————

One 15-ounce can **cannellini beans**, drained + rinsed

1½ cups whole milk + more as needed

2½ cups boxed pancake mix (see note)

1 tablespoon unsalted butter + more as needed

1 Process the beans and milk in a blender until smooth, then transfer to a large bowl. Stir in the pancake mix (if the brand you're using calls for eggs or oil, omit them) until the ingredients are just combined and pourable, but still thick (it's okay if the mixture is a little lumpy). You will likely need to add more milk; how much milk depends on your mix, but I often add another ¼ to ¾ cup—enough to make the batter pourable but still on the thicker side, as too much milk can yield a pancake that's *too* moist.

FOR PANCAKES: Melt the butter in a large skillet over medium-low heat. Once the pan is hot, pour about ⅓ cup of the batter into the pan; this will make one 4-inch pancake. Cook the batter until bubbles start to pop on the pancake's surface and the pan side is golden brown, then flip the pancake and cook it until the other side is also golden brown—3 to 5 minutes per side. It's important to cook the pancakes low and slow to ensure their insides dry out a bit and are not too moist. Repeat with the remainder of the batter, adding more butter as needed to prevent the pancakes from sticking to the pan—and because butter is delicious!

FOR WAFFLES: Melt the butter and use it to brush the inside of a preheated waffle iron; alternatively, you can spray the

CONTINUED . . .

. . . CONTINUED

waffle iron with cooking oil spray. Add approximately ½ cup of the batter (or however much is appropriate for your machine), cooking the waffles until they are crisp and brown—about 5 minutes. You want them on the darker/crispier side to make sure the insides dry out a little.

2 Serve with your favorite toppings (we like extra butter, syrup, and fruit)!

STORE IT + FREEZE IT

Pancakes and waffles will stay good in the fridge for up to a week and in the freezer for up to 5 months. Thaw from frozen by baking at 350°F for 10 minutes or microwaving on high for 1 to 1½ minutes (waffles reheat best in the oven). You can also heat them from the freezer or fridge by putting them directly into your toaster!

NOTE

*I have found the best results with pancake mixes that are **not** labeled as "complete" mixes. Brands that are labeled "complete" (for which water is the only ingredient you add) often contain powdered milk and eggs, making them a bit too moist.*

SWAP IT

Any white bean will work as a substitute for the cannellini beans.

white beans

zucchini
replaces
the milk!

zucchini french toast

I try to keep my recipes as simple as possible while still making them mind-blowingly delicious. And I couldn't ask you to go from spending 5 minutes on French toast to 35 minutes. So I tested and retested and found the perfect solution for a veggie French toast that's just as fast and easy as the original. The trick is to use zucchini to replace the milk—its high water content gives you all the moisture you need. So blend up some eggs, zucchini, and seasonings and have yourself an awesome French toast breakfast. After one bite, I bet you'll ask yourself why you *wouldn't* always make French toast with zucchini!

―――――― MAKES 4 THICK OR 6 THIN SLICES OF FRENCH TOAST ――――――

4 large eggs

½ small **zucchini** (2½ ounces), peeled + coarsely chopped (½ cup)

1 tablespoon honey

1 teaspoon ground cinnamon

1 teaspoon vanilla extract

Kosher salt

4 large or 6 small slices bread

1 tablespoon unsalted butter

1 Blend the eggs, zucchini, honey, cinnamon, vanilla, and a pinch of salt in a blender or food processor until the mixture is smooth with no chunks remaining, then transfer it to a large bowl. Submerge the bread slices in the mixture, coating both sides.

2 Heat a large skillet or griddle over medium heat and melt the butter in the pan. Working in batches if necessary, arrange the bread slices in the pan and cook until they are golden brown on both sides and still moist, but not wet in the center—about 3 minutes per side. To keep finished French toast warm as you work, place cooked slices on a wire rack set on a baking sheet and place in an oven set to 200°F.

SERVING SUGGESTION
To serve, top with maple syrup, butter, and berries if desired.

NOTE
If you want to use challah bread (pictured), a double batch of batter should be perfect for one loaf of challah bread French toast.

FREEZE IT
Put completely cooled French toast in a food storage bag and freeze for up to 5 months. To thaw, bake in your oven at 350°F for 8 to 10 minutes or microwave on high for 20 to 30 seconds. You can also put the frozen slices directly into the toaster. Before freezing, I often cut the French toast into strips for easy dipping and easier portioning for kid meals.

EVEN MORE VEGGIES
Don't mind a green look? Leave the skin on the zucchini for added nutrition with no difference in taste. Additionally, ½ cup steamed or canned carrots (8.25-ounce can) works great as a swap for the zucchini.

cauliflower oatmeal

Oatmeal has always been a go-to breakfast in my house. And I couldn't be happier when my kids devour a bowl of oats. Though oats alone are great, adding cauliflower really makes this an all-star breakfast. It's as simple as throwing some cauliflower rice in with your water/milk. You can even use your favorite packet of oatmeal for this recipe (check out my Hack It note).

SERVES 2

Heat the milk, 1 cup water, cauliflower rice (no need to thaw if frozen), and salt in a small pot over high heat. Bring the mixture to a boil, then reduce it to a simmer and cook until the cauliflower is mostly softened—2 to 3 minutes. Add the oats and continue to simmer until the oatmeal is soft and thick—about 6 minutes more. Serve hot.

SERVING SUGGESTION

Finish off with your favorite toppings, or follow my daughter Ivy's lead and top with her favorite combo of dried cranberries, honey, ground cinnamon, and hemp seeds.

HACK IT

Have a favorite packet of oatmeal? Add some cauliflower! Stovetop: Simmer ½ cup water or milk with ¼ cup cauliflower rice (no need to thaw if frozen) until the rice is very soft—3 to 4 minutes. Add the packet of oatmeal and let the mixture sit until thick—about 1 minute. Microwave: Microwave ½ cup water or milk with ¼ cup cauliflower rice (no need to thaw if frozen) for 2 minutes on high, add your packet, and continue to cook for 1 minute more. It's that simple!

1 cup whole milk

½ cup **cauliflower rice**, fresh or frozen

½ teaspoon kosher salt

1 cup old-fashioned rolled oats

carrot apple oatmeal

In less than 7 minutes, you could be eating *this*: creamy oats with flecks of carrot made warm and toasty with the addition of vanilla and topped with cinnamon–brown sugar apples. It feels *so* indulgent, but really there's only 1 tablespoon of added sugar! When your morning starts this way, you know it's going to be a good day.

— SERVES 2 —

1 cup whole milk

1 cup old-fashioned rolled oats

1 medium **carrot** (2½ ounces), shredded (¾ cup)

1 teaspoon vanilla extract

Kosher salt

2 tablespoons unsalted butter

1 apple, peeled, cored, and cut into ¼-inch cubes (1 cup)

2 tablespoons packed brown sugar

1 teaspoon ground cinnamon

Greek yogurt, for a garnish (optional)

1 Heat the milk, 1 cup water, oats, carrot, vanilla, and a pinch of salt in a medium saucepan over high heat. Bring this mixture to a boil, then reduce the heat to medium-low and simmer until all the water is absorbed, stirring occasionally—5 to 7 minutes.

2 While the oats cook, melt the butter in a small pan over medium-high heat. Add the apple and cook until it just begins to soften—about 5 minutes. Then add the brown sugar, cinnamon, and a pinch of salt. Stir this mixture to coat the apples and continue cooking until the sugar has melted and the apples are soft—2 to 3 minutes more.

3 To serve, divide the oatmeal between two bowls and top each bowl with half of the apple mixture and a dollop of Greek yogurt (if desired).

banana carrot oatmeal muffins

I call these "oatmeal muffins" because they are basically a bowl of carrot and banana oatmeal baked and served in muffin form. It's a grab-and-go breakfast, which I always appreciate as I run out the door late (again!) for school drop-off. On top of being convenient, they are hearty and filling and taste exactly like banana bread. I have yet to have one of my kids say no to them (even when I turn them green—see the Even More Veggies! tip). Plus, they're silly easy to make; you dump everything into your food processor, blend, pour, and bake. A super easy recipe with a big payoff? Yes, please!

MAKES 12 REGULAR MUFFINS OR 48 MINI MUFFINS

3 cups old-fashioned rolled oats

2 medium **carrots** (5 ounces), chopped (1 cup)

½ cup **wheat germ**

3 medium bananas

¼–½ cup maple syrup (see note)

2 large eggs

2 teaspoons baking powder

2 teaspoons ground cinnamon

1 teaspoon vanilla extract

½ teaspoon kosher salt

Chocolate chips (optional)

1 Preheat the oven to 350°F. Spray a 12-cup standard muffin tin (or two mini muffin tins) generously with cooking oil spray, or line with paper liners sprayed with cooking oil spray.

2 Process the oats, carrots, and wheat germ in a food processor (a blender does work, but requires extra stirring/scraping) until everything is very finely chopped. Add the bananas, maple syrup, eggs, baking powder, cinnamon, vanilla, and salt, and let the food processor run for 1 to 2 minutes, until the mixture is batter-like and mostly smooth (the oats will never be completely smooth, but everything else should be).

3 Pour the batter evenly into the cups of the muffin tin(s), filling each cup to the top (these muffins don't rise as much as other muffins). Sprinkle the tops of the muffins with chocolate chips (if desired).

4 Bake the muffins until their tops are dry and medium brown; these benefit from a little extra baking to dry out the centers—25 to 30 minutes for regular muffins and 20 to 25 minutes for mini muffins. Let the muffins cool completely before eating.

NOTE

The amount of syrup depends on the ripeness of your bananas. If your bananas are very ripe, use ¼ cup syrup; if they are medium ripe, ⅓ cup syrup; and if they are underripe, ½ cup syrup.

SWAP IT

Replace the wheat germ with ½ cup of any of the following: more oats, whole wheat flour, or ground flaxseed.

FREEZE IT

Freeze muffins for up to 5 months. To thaw, microwave for 1 to 1½ minutes or bake at 350°F for 8 to 10 minutes.

EVEN MORE VEGGIES!

Think your kids might be ready to accept that green can be great? You can add a whole package of frozen spinach to this recipe and it will taste exactly the same, while of course becoming very green— and even more nutritious. Thaw a 10-ounce package of spinach and squeeze out as much liquid as you possibly can. Then add the spinach along with ½ cup more oats (3½ cups oats total) to the food processor with everything else.

strawberry cheesecake chia seed pudding

Chia seeds are amazing little things. There are massive amounts of nutrients crammed into these tiny packages. They are bursting with high-quality protein and fiber; contain large amounts of antioxidants, calcium, and magnesium; and are the richest plant source of omega-3 fatty acids. The bottom line is that they are really stinking good for you. And because they absorb up to 10 times their weight in liquid (I know, right?), if you add them to this creamy strawberry mixture, they swell up into an energy-packed pudding that just might give you the fuel you need to finally get in that early-morning workout . . . or you could just sleep—sleep is pretty amazing too.

—— SERVES 4 ——

2 cups strawberries, fresh or thawed from frozen (10 ounces), sliced + more for a garnish

1 cup plain Greek yogurt or cottage cheese (8 ounces)

½ cup milk

¼ cup honey

⅓ cup **chia seeds** (1¾ ounces)

Whipped cream or yogurt, for a garnish

4 crunchy cinnamon-brown sugar breakfast biscuits, such as Belvita

SWAP IT
Replace the plain yogurt or cottage cheese with your favorite flavored yogurt; because the flavored yogurt is sweetened, you can use just 2 tablespoons honey or none at all.

1 Blend the strawberries, yogurt or cottage cheese, milk, and honey in a blender until the mixture is completely smooth. Add the chia seeds and pulse until they are just mixed in but still whole.

2 Divide the mixture among 4 small mason jars or bowls by adding about ¾ cup to each container, then cover with the lid or plastic wrap. Refrigerate until the mixture has thickened to the texture of pudding—at least 2 hours, but preferably overnight.

3 To serve, top the pudding with extra strawberries and a dollop of whipped cream or yogurt, then crumble one of the breakfast biscuits over each serving and dig in!

real pumpkin
inside

pumpkin pie granola

We all love granola. Ivy loves granola for her cereal in the morning, I eat it throughout the day (basically every time I walk by it in the kitchen), and it's the perfect thing for a lunch box. This granola is a touch sweet, with warm pumpkin pie spices and vanilla. My favorite part is that you can make it into cereal or into big clusters for snacking, and many of the ingredients can be subbed out for whatever you have on hand. After you customize and cook this up, you can feel good that it will stay crunchy and perfect for forever on your counter. Best of all, there is actual pumpkin in it!

———————————————————— MAKES 10 CUPS ————————————————————

1 cup pure **pumpkin** puree (9 ounces)

½ cup maple syrup

½ cup packed brown sugar

½ cup unsalted butter (1 stick), melted

1 large egg white

2 teaspoons pumpkin pie spice

2 teaspoons vanilla extract

1 teaspoon kosher salt

5 cups old-fashioned rolled oats (1 pound)

1½ cups finely chopped pecans (5 ounces)

1 cup dried cranberries (5 ounces)

¾ cup **wheat germ**

1 Preheat the oven to 275°F. In a large bowl, whisk the pumpkin puree, maple syrup, brown sugar, butter, egg white, pumpkin pie spice, vanilla, and salt until combined. Add the oats, pecans, cranberries, and wheat germ, and stir until all ingredients are well incorporated and the oats and nuts are completely coated in the pumpkin mixture.

2 FOR BREAKFAST CEREAL GRANOLA (SMALLER CLUSTERS): Line two large, rimmed baking sheets with parchment paper. Divide the granola mixture between the two baking sheets, spreading it out evenly in a single layer. Bake until the top of the mixture is dry—about 30 minutes. Remove the granola from the oven and use a flat metal spatula to gently stir it, then return the sheets to the oven, rotating their positions. Continue baking until the mixture is completely dry and the oats and nuts are toasted—30 to 60 minutes more. (How long it takes to dry out and toast can vary a bit, and you want to keep an eye on it after 30 minutes; it can go from golden brown to burnt fast!) Remove the granola from the oven and allow it to cool completely on the baking sheets (it will crisp as it cools). Once the granola has cooled, break it into smaller clusters.

FOR SNACKING GRANOLA (LARGER CLUSTERS): Line one large, rimmed baking sheet with parchment paper. Transfer the granola mixture to the prepared baking sheet, spreading it out evenly in a single layer, pressing gently so that it covers the entire baking sheet. Bake until the top of the mixture is dry—about 1 hour 15 minutes. Remove the granola from the oven and use a flat metal spatula to carefully flip large pieces

CONTINUED . . .

of the granola over (it should remain mostly in large slabs), then return the pan to the oven. Continue baking, rotating the baking sheet halfway through, until the granola is completely dry and darkened in color—45 to 75 minutes more. Remove the granola from the oven and allow it to cool completely on the baking sheet (it will crisp even more as it cools). Once the granola has cooled, break it into large clusters.

STORE IT

The granola will last on your countertop for at least 3 weeks.

SWAP IT

Replace the pecans with any nut, or nix them and add an additional 1 cup oats instead. You can also replace the wheat germ with ¾ cup ground flaxseed or ¾ cup more oats. And feel free to sub the pumpkin pie spice with cinnamon or simply omit.

NOTE

Use the leftover canned pumpkin to make my Caramel Pumpkin Cake Bars (page 217), and use leftover wheat germ in my Eggplant Chicken Tenders (page 82).

zucchini biscuits

I fell in love with biscuits about the same time I fell in love with my BFF, Damaris Phillips. Getting to know more about her and her Southern roots meant getting to know about biscuits. After hearing her talk about them for the 645th time, I finally took the plunge and was *shocked* at just how easy they were to make, especially when I got out the food processor. And when I realized you could freeze biscuits and then pull out just one at a time for a fresh flaky treat whenever, I was even more sold. Damaris never did hers with zucchini, but she's a veggie lover too, so I know she'll love these as much as I do.

———————————— MAKES 8 BISCUITS ————————————

½ cup cold or frozen unsalted butter (1 stick) + 2 tablespoons for basting

1 medium **zucchini** (7 ounces), peeled + coarsely chopped (1½ cups)

¾ cup + ¼ cup heavy cream or half-and-half (½ pint total), divided

3 cups all-purpose flour

1 tablespoon baking powder

1 tablespoon granulated sugar

1½ teaspoons kosher salt

1 Preheat the oven to 425°F. Cut the ½ cup cold butter into ½-inch pieces (cubes are best if you'll mix your dough with a food processor), or grate with a cheese grater (this is the way to go if mixing by hand and works best with frozen butter). Once the butter is chopped or grated, refrigerate it to keep it as cold as possible until needed. Blend the zucchini and ¾ cup of the heavy cream or half-and-half in a blender until the mixture is very smooth. (Avoid overblending or you will end up with zucchini whipped cream. However, if the mixture does get a little fluffy, don't panic! It should still fold in just fine.) You should have 1½ cups total liquid when finished; if you don't, add more heavy cream, half-and-half, or even water to reach 1½ cups. Refrigerate the zucchini-cream mixture until needed.

2 Prepare a baking sheet with parchment paper or cooking oil spray.

BY HAND: Stir the flour, baking powder, sugar, and salt in a medium bowl to combine. Add the cold grated butter and stir until the mixture resembles coarse meal; you want to work fast so the butter does not melt. Add the zucchini-cream mixture and stir until the ingredients are just combined, being sure not to overwork the dough.

FOOD PROCESSOR: Pulse the flour, baking powder, sugar, and salt together, then add the cubed butter and pulse again until the mixture resembles coarse meal. Add the zucchini-cream mixture and pulse until the mixture is just combined.

CONTINUED . . .

3 Knead the dough on a floured surface five or six times until it has a uniform consistency. Add more flour to the surface, then roll the dough out into a 1½-inch-thick disk. Cut out the biscuits using a 2½-inch biscuit cutter (you can also make square biscuits by cutting them out with a knife). When you cut, be sure to cut straight up and down without twisting the cutter; dip the cutter or knife in flour repeatedly to keep it from sticking. Knead the scraps together, reroll, and cut more biscuits until all the dough has been used; the biscuits that come from this reroll might not be the prettiest, but they'll still be delicious.

4 Transfer the dough rounds carefully to the prepared baking sheet without pressing on their sides, placing them close together (about ½ inch apart) in order to help them rise.

5 Baste the tops of the biscuits with the remaining ¼ cup heavy cream or half-and-half (this actually makes them brown better than butter). Bake them on a high rack in the oven until they are fluffy and golden brown on top—15 to 20 minutes.

6 While the biscuits bake, melt the remaining 2 tablespoons butter. Remove the biscuits from the oven and baste them with the butter.

SERVING SUGGESTION

Serve with my Strawberry + Chia Jam (page 90) and, of course, some extra butter.

EVEN MORE VEGGIES!

Leave the skin on the zucchini if you don't mind some specks of green in your flaky butter biscuits.

FREEZE IT

After Step 4, place the entire baking sheet of raw dough rounds in the freezer, allowing the rounds to freeze without touching, then transfer them to a food storage bag. Store frozen for up to 5 months. When you're ready to enjoy, bake as the recipe directs at 425°F, but for 18 to 20 minutes. Sometimes I bake them all at once and sometimes I bake up just three—for me, myself, and I.

zucchini

carrot biscuits

Not everyone loves raw carrots, but foods with carrots baked into them are a different story. Take carrot cake, for example—when you bite into it, you aren't overwhelmed with carrot taste, and with all the other yummy flavors and textures in there, you might forget carrots are even involved. The same goes for these biscuits. Add a little sprinkle of cinnamon sugar, and you've got a sweet, crunchy topping that contrasts with and complements the savoriness of the biscuits. They remind me of carrot cake, while still being totally appropriate for breakfast.

—————— MAKES 8 BISCUITS ——————

½ cup cold or frozen unsalted butter (1 stick) + 2 tablespoons for basting

1 cup **carrot juice**, chilled

½ cup heavy cream

3 cups all-purpose flour

1 tablespoon baking powder

1 tablespoon packed brown sugar

1½ teaspoons kosher salt

TOPPING

¼ cup packed brown sugar

½ teaspoon ground cinnamon

1 Preheat the oven to 425°F. Cut the ½ cup cold butter into ½-inch pieces (cubes are best if you'll mix your dough with a food processor), or grate it with a cheese grater (this is the way to go if mixing by hand and works best with frozen butter). Once the butter is chopped or grated, refrigerate it to keep it as cold as possible until needed. In a small bowl, combine the carrot juice and cream, then refrigerate this mixture as well until needed.

2 Prepare a baking sheet with parchment paper or cooking oil spray.

BY HAND: Combine the flour, baking powder, 1 tablespoon brown sugar, and salt in a medium bowl using a whisk. Add the grated cold butter to the mixture and stir until the mixture resembles coarse meal; you want to work fast so the butter does not melt. Pour in the carrot juice–cream mixture. Stir until the ingredients are just combined, being sure not to overwork the dough.

FOOD PROCESSOR: Pulse the flour, baking powder, 1 tablespoon brown sugar, and salt together, then add the cubed butter and pulse again until you get a mixture that resembles coarse meal. Add the carrot juice–cream mixture and pulse until the mixture is just combined.

3 Knead the dough on a floured surface five or six times, until it has a uniform consistency. Add more flour to the surface, then roll it out into a 1½-inch-thick disk. Cut out the biscuits using a 2½-inch biscuit cutter (you can also make square biscuits by cutting them out with a knife). When you cut, be sure to cut straight up and down without twisting the

CONTINUED . . .

cutter; dip the cutter or knife in flour to keep it from sticking. Knead the scraps together, reroll, and cut more biscuits until all the dough has been used; these "second round" ones might not be the prettiest, but they'll still be delicious.

4 Transfer the dough rounds carefully to the prepared baking sheet without pressing on their sides, placing them close together (about ½ inch apart) in order to help them get extra big and fluffy.

5 Melt the remaining 2 tablespoons of butter. Combine the ¼ cup sugar and the cinnamon in a small bowl.

6 Baste the tops of the biscuits with the melted butter and sprinkle each biscuit with 1 to 1½ teaspoons of the cinnamon-sugar mixture. Bake until they are fluffy and lightly golden brown—about 15 minutes.

NOTE

Freeze leftover carrot juice in an ice cube tray for next time, or use in my Oat + Cheddar Cheese Crackers (page 194) or Buffalo Party Mix (page 198). You can also make your own carrot juice by blending 1 cup chopped carrots and 1 cup water together. After blending, strain through a fine-mesh sieve, pushing on the carrot pulp to extract as much juice as possible. This juice will not be as concentrated as store-bought carrot juice, but it's still a great substitute.

FREEZE IT

In Step 6, after topping with the cinnamon-sugar mixture and before baking, place the entire baking sheet of raw dough rounds in the freezer, allowing the rounds to freeze without touching, then transfer them to a food storage bag. Store frozen for up to 5 months. When you're ready to enjoy, bake as the recipe directs at 425°F, but for 18 to 20 minutes. You can bake them all or bake up just one for yourself before everyone gets out of bed; it's the best way to start a hectic day.

vanilla yogurt coffee cake muffins

People always want to know the secret ingredient—what was it that transformed the dish from good to *spectacular*? Well, it's time for me to let you in on the mystery of my favorite muffins *ever*. Drumroll, please . . . it's beans and yogurt! Believe it or not, they are the keys to an incredibly airy and light muffin with the most decadent vanilla flavor. And because I just can't help myself, I've added a streusel topping for a kick of sweetness and a pop of crunch that takes these ultra-moist muffins one step beyond perfection. The secret is out, I've spilled the beans . . . literally. Get it? #LameMomJokes

——————— MAKES 12 REGULAR MUFFINS OR 48 MINI MUFFINS ———————

STREUSEL TOPPING

½ cup all-purpose flour

⅓ cup very finely chopped pecans (1¾ ounces; optional)

¼ cup packed brown sugar

4 tablespoons unsalted butter, melted

½ teaspoon ground cinnamon

⅛ teaspoon kosher salt

MUFFINS

1½ cups all-purpose flour

½ cup packed brown sugar

2 teaspoons baking powder

½ teaspoon baking soda

½ teaspoon ground cinnamon

¼ teaspoon kosher salt

One 15-ounce can **cannellini beans**, drained + rinsed

1 cup vanilla yogurt (8 ounces; see note)

4 tablespoons unsalted butter, melted

1 large egg

TO MAKE THE STREUSEL TOPPING:

In a medium bowl, use your hands to squeeze together the flour, pecans, brown sugar, butter, cinnamon, and salt until the mixture becomes crumbly (if you'd rather not use pecans here, just add an extra ¼ cup flour to the mixture). Allow the topping to chill in the refrigerator while you make the muffins.

TO MAKE THE MUFFINS:

1 Preheat the oven to 400°F. Spray a 12-cup standard muffin tin (or two mini muffin tins) generously with cooking oil spray, or line with paper liners sprayed with cooking oil spray.

2 In a large bowl, combine the flour, brown sugar, baking powder, baking soda, cinnamon, and salt, whisking to combine.

3 Blend the cannellini beans, yogurt, butter, and egg in a blender or food processor until the mixture is completely smooth.

CONTINUED . . .

Add it to the bowl with the flour mixture, folding until just combined (the batter will be very thick).

4 Divide the batter among the prepared muffin cups, filling each cup to almost full. Sprinkle the top of each muffin generously with about 2 tablespoons of the chilled Streusel Topping. Bake the muffins, rotating the muffin tin(s) once halfway through the baking time, until they are puffed and golden brown and a toothpick inserted in the center of one comes out clean—18 to 22 minutes, and for mini muffins 8 to 12 minutes.

5 Allow the muffins to cool for 5 minutes in the muffin tins, then transfer them to a cooling rack and allow them to cool completely.

FREEZE IT

Store these in an airtight plastic bag in your freezer for up to 5 months. To thaw, leave full-size muffins at room temperature for 2 hours or microwave for 45 seconds on high. Allow mini muffins to thaw for 1 hour at room temperature or microwave for 20 to 30 seconds on high.

NOTES

* *When I'm too tired to stand I make these a little simpler with no crumble topping and instead sprinkle with a little brown sugar and cinnamon. They are equally as delicious and a little less messy for the lunchbox.*
* *I prefer full-fat non-Greek yogurt, but any vanilla yogurt works, even Greek yogurt.*
* *Egg allergy? Simply lose the egg and add a splash more milk to the batter to thin it a little. The protein from the beans will hold it together fine.*

SWAP IT

You can replace the cannellini beans with any white bean—great northern beans, navy beans, butter beans, and so on.

white
beans

5 cups of spinach

double chocolate chip muffins

top ten

There may be a moment when you look at a blender full of spinach and avocado and wonder if making this recipe was really a good idea. Keep the faith, bake these muffins, and when they are just cool enough to eat, you'll take your first bite and experience the most incredibly moist, fluffy muffin, complete with chunks of melty chocolate. And as you close your eyes, reveling in the moment, you may have to remind yourself about that blender full of veggies. Because all you'll taste is chocolate, lots of dreamy rich chocolate.

—————— MAKES 12 REGULAR MUFFINS OR 48 MINI MUFFINS ——————

5 cups **baby spinach** (5 ounces)

½ cup whole milk + more as needed

½ small ripe **avocado** (1¼ ounces), mashed (¼ cup)

¼ cup canola or avocado oil

1 large egg

1½ teaspoons vanilla extract

1⅔ cups all-purpose flour

⅔ cup unsweetened cocoa powder

⅔ cup packed brown sugar

1½ teaspoons baking powder

½ teaspoon baking soda

¼ teaspoon kosher salt

1 cup + ¼ cup semisweet chocolate chips (6 ounces total), divided

1 Preheat the oven to 350°F. Spray a 12-cup standard muffin tin (or two mini muffin tins) generously with cooking oil spray, or line with paper liners sprayed with cooking oil spray.

2 Blend the spinach, milk, avocado, oil, egg, and vanilla in a blender until the mixture is very smooth and you don't see pieces of spinach, just green milk. If you are having trouble blending because the mixture is too thick, add a splash more milk.

3 In a large bowl, whisk the flour, cocoa powder, brown sugar, baking powder, baking soda, and salt until they are combined, then stir in the spinach mixture. It's fine for the batter to be thick, but if it's so thick you are having trouble combining add a splash more milk. Fold in 1 cup of the chocolate chips until they are just incorporated.

4 Pour the batter into the prepared muffin cups, filling them almost to the top. Sprinkle the muffins with the remaining ¼ cup chocolate chips. Bake the muffins, rotating the muffin tin(s) once halfway through the

CONTINUED . . .

step 2   step 3   step 4

. . . CONTINUED

baking time, until they puff up and a toothpick inserted into the center of a muffin comes out clean—for regular-sized muffins about 20 minutes, and for mini muffins 10 to 13 minutes.

5 Allow the muffins to cool for 5 minutes before removing them from the tin, then transfer the muffins to a cooling rack. Once cool enough to eat, devour!

FREEZE IT

Seal the muffins in an airtight plastic bag and store in your freezer for up to 5 months. To thaw, leave full-size muffins at room temperature for 2 hours or microwave for 45 seconds on high. Allow mini muffins to thaw at room temperature for 1 hour or microwave for 20 to 30 seconds on high.

SWAP IT

For added fiber, replace ⅔ cup of the all-purpose flour with whole wheat flour (for a total of 1 cup all-purpose flour + ⅔ cup whole wheat flour). Avocado not ripe? Skip it and add more oil instead, ⅓ cup total canola or avocado oil. If the batter is on the extra thick side for this non-avocado version, add a splash more milk.

yellow squash

lemon blueberry muffins

Lemon blueberry muffins—just saying those words makes me smile. I picture a quiet, early morning when I come down to the kitchen before the kids are up and see these on my counter. I unwrap one and take a bright, lemony bite, savoring the pop of sweet blueberries . . .

Snapping back to reality, I can already hear you asking, "But, um . . . do these have squash in them?" They do! Yellow squash plays a role in these muffins similar to zucchini in zucchini bread. It keeps them moist and delicately melts away into the batter, so you get that same great muffin texture and taste—and you're eating veggies before noon. How can you have a bad day when it starts like this?

MAKES 12 REGULAR MUFFINS OR 48 MINI MUFFINS

1 medium **yellow squash** (8 ounces)

2 cups all-purpose flour

2 teaspoons baking powder

½ teaspoon baking soda

¼ teaspoon kosher salt

¾ cup granulated sugar + more for sprinkling

⅔ cup plain Greek yogurt (5.3 ounces)

4 tablespoons unsalted butter, melted

2 large eggs

Juice + zest of 2 small lemons

1 teaspoon vanilla extract

1 cup blueberries (6 ounces)

1 Preheat the oven to 375°F. Spray a 12-cup standard muffin tin (or two mini muffin tins) generously with cooking oil spray, or line with paper liners sprayed with cooking oil spray.

2 Use the large holes on a box grater to grate the yellow squash, then set aside (this should give you about 1¾ cups grated squash, lightly packed; no need to squeeze the squash).

3 In a medium bowl, whisk the flour, baking powder, baking soda, and salt until combined, then set aside.

4 In a large bowl, combine the sugar, yogurt, butter, eggs, lemon juice, lemon zest, and vanilla, whisking until smooth. Add the flour mixture and, switching to a spoon, stir to create a mostly smooth batter; it will be thick, but that's okay. Stir in the grated squash until just combined, then gently fold in the blueberries.

5 Divide the batter among the prepared muffin cups, filling the cups until they are almost full. Sprinkle the tops of the muffins with extra sugar. Bake the muffins until they are medium brown on top (don't be afraid to get some color on them)—25 to 35 minutes for regular muffins and 12 to 17 minutes for mini muffins.

6 Allow the muffins to cool for 5 minutes in the muffin tin, then transfer them to a cooling rack and allow them to cool completely. Finally, *eat!*

CONTINUED . . .

step 4

step 5

step 6

. . . CONTINUED

FREEZE IT

Store in an airtight plastic bag in your freezer for up to 5 months. To thaw, leave full-size muffins at room temperature for 2 hours or microwave for 45 seconds on high. Allow mini muffins to thaw at room temperature for 1 hour or microwave for 20 to 30 seconds on high.

SWAP IT

You can sub in zucchini for the yellow squash; there may be a few specks of green, but nothing that will bother most kids—especially once they take a bite and discover how awesome these muffins are.

acorn squash bread

Pumpkin bread, zucchini bread—both fine. But Acorn Squash Bread is where my love lies. This is one of my favorite things to give to family and friends. To make gifting easy, you can bake it in a disposable paper pan or remove it from your regular baking pan and wrap it in parchment paper, securing with some kitchen twine. Watch out, though, after tasting this people will be knocking down your door for more.

MAKES ONE 9 × 5-INCH LOAF (ABOUT 8 SLICES)

1 small **acorn squash**
  (about 1 pound)
2 tablespoons olive oil
½ teaspoon + ½ teaspoon
  kosher salt, divided
1⅔ cups all-purpose flour
1 teaspoon ground
  cinnamon
1 teaspoon baking soda
½ teaspoon baking powder
¼ teaspoon ground nutmeg
¼ teaspoon ground cloves
¾ cup packed brown sugar
⅓ cup granulated sugar
½ cup canola or avocado oil
⅓ cup apple cider
2 large eggs
1 teaspoon vanilla extract

TOPPING

1 cup powdered sugar
1–5 tablespoons apple cider
⅓ cup granola

1 Preheat the oven to 425°F. Acorn squash is a wobbly ball that wants to roll around, so to safely cut, first slice off the bottom end (the end with no stem) to create a flat base. Then you can cut it in half lengthwise much more easily. Use a soupspoon to scoop out the seeds and discard them. Arrange the squash cut-side-up on a rimmed baking sheet. Drizzle it with the olive oil and ½ teaspoon of the salt. Bake the squash until its flesh can easily be pierced with a fork—about 45 minutes.

2 Remove the squash from the oven, reduce the oven temperature to 350°F, and grease a 9 × 5-inch loaf pan. Scoop the flesh of the squash into the bowl of a food processor (discard the skins) and puree until smooth; this should give you 1 cup puree.

3 In a large bowl, whisk together the flour, cinnamon, baking soda, baking powder, nutmeg, and cloves. In a second large

CONTINUED . . .

bowl, whisk together the squash puree, brown sugar, granulated sugar, oil, ⅓ cup apple cider, eggs, vanilla, and remaining ½ teaspoon salt.

4 Pour the wet mixture into the dry ingredients and stir until just combined. Then pour the batter into the prepared loaf pan and bake until the edges of the bread are brown and a toothpick inserted into its center comes out clean—55 to 65 minutes. Let the bread cool in the pan for 15 minutes, then remove it from the pan and allow it to cool completely on a wire rack.

5 For the topping, whisk together the powdered sugar and 1 tablespoon apple cider until a smooth glaze forms, adding more cider, 1 tablespoon at a time, if it is too thick. Drizzle over the cooled bread, sprinkle with the granola, and serve.

FOR MUFFINS

To make muffins, divide the batter among 12 cups of a lined or greased muffin tin and bake at 350°F until the edges are brown and a toothpick inserted in the center comes out clean—20 to 25 minutes. Let cool in the pan for a few minutes, then transfer to a rack to cool completely. Drizzle the cooled muffins with the glaze and sprinkle with granola.

SWAP IT

Apple juice can be used instead of apple cider in the bread and glaze, or you can simply use milk or water. You can also replace the acorn squash with 1 cup canned pure pumpkin puree.

MORE VEGGIES AT LUNCH

If it's lunchtime, I'm scrambling! Somehow, the day gets away from me and I'm suddenly surprised that I have to prepare yet another meal—all while hungry kids remind me just how hungry they are on repeat. And when we're talking school lunch prep, well, I have yet to allot more than 2½ minutes for that task. So you'll find many of these lunch recipes are easy make-aheads, providing quick fixes that can always be kept on hand. And since I've whipped up more PB+Js than might seem humanly possible, I've figured out how to make them more nutritious (adding hummus to peanut butter is actually much more delicious than it sounds). In the end, it all equals a more successful midday meal and maybe even enough time to finally drink that tea you've warmed up four times already.

souped-up broccoli cheddar

Broccoli cheddar soup was already doing a decent job in the veggie department, but let's face it—the broccoli has always seemed a little lonely in this creamy, cheesy soup, don't you think? Not anymore! We're giving broccoli three veggie friends. Pureed zucchini, carrots, and onion are joining the festivities, making the base of this soup even more creamy and rich. Throw in some Parm and seasonings to bump everything up a notch and you've got a true party on your hands (or should I say "taste buds"?).

MAKES 6 CUPS; SERVES 4

1 tablespoon + 4 tablespoons unsalted butter, divided

1 medium **zucchini** (9 ounces), chopped (2 cups)

1 medium yellow **onion** (8 ounces), chopped (1½ cups)

2 medium **carrots** (5 ounces), finely chopped (1 cup)

4 garlic cloves, sliced

Kosher salt

1 cup + 2 cups chicken stock, divided

¼ cup all-purpose flour

2 cups whole milk

1 head **broccoli** (10 ounces), florets finely chopped (2 cups)

1 teaspoon mustard powder

1 teaspoon paprika

½ teaspoon garlic powder

2 cups shredded cheddar cheese (8 ounces)

¼ cup grated Parmesan cheese (1 ounce)

Ground black pepper

1 Melt 1 tablespoon of the butter in a large pot over medium heat. Add the zucchini, onion, carrots, garlic, and 1 teaspoon salt. Sauté the veggies until they are mostly tender—about 10 minutes. Add 1 cup of the chicken stock, bring to a simmer, and continue cooking until the veggies are very tender and easily broken up with your spoon—about 15 minutes more. Carefully transfer the mixture to a blender along with the remaining 2 cups stock and puree until smooth. Do not clean out the pot.

2 In the pot, over medium heat, melt the remaining 4 tablespoons butter. Whisk in the flour until smooth. Cook the mixture for 2 minutes. Slowly add the milk, whisking well until there are no clumps, then bring to a simmer; once the sauce has thickened, stir in the pureed veggies.

3 Add the broccoli, mustard powder, paprika, garlic powder, and another 1 teaspoon salt and stir to combine. Cook until the broccoli is tender and the soup has reached your desired thickness—20 to 30 minutes. If the soup is too thick, add more stock or water; if too thin, continue cooking until it thickens up.

4 Stir in the cheddar and Parmesan; taste and add more salt if needed (I often add an extra ½ teaspoon). Serve hot topped with pepper.

zucchini + carrots

chicken noodle soup

My Ivy loves the idea of soup—for whatever reason, she finds it very exciting (probably there was a *Paw Patrol* episode about how soup is awesome). However, she's only actually interested in eating soup that contains nothing more than broth and her favorite ABC noodles. She will pick at the celery and chicken, and a piece of carrot does occasionally hit her lips, but I love this recipe because incorporating pureed veggies as part of the broth ensures she's getting them in every bite, all while making the broth even more flavorful. I think even the Paw Patrol would approve.

— SERVES 8 —

One 12-ounce package egg noodles

4 tablespoons unsalted butter

1 pound **carrots** (5 medium carrots), finely chopped (3 cups)

1 pound **celery** (1 bunch), chopped (4 cups)

1 medium yellow **onion** (8 ounces), chopped (1½ cups)

4 garlic cloves, minced

1 tablespoon minced fresh thyme leaves + more for a garnish

Kosher salt

Ground black pepper

2 quarts (8 cups) chicken stock (see note)

¾ pound cooked chicken, cubed or shredded

1 Place a large pot of salted water over high heat for cooking the egg noodles. When the water boils, add the egg noodles and cook according to the package directions. When done, drain and set aside. If not using immediately, add a splash of olive oil to prevent the noodles from sticking as they sit.

2 Heat the butter in a large pot over medium-high heat, then add the carrots and cook until they are slightly softened—about 10 minutes. Add the celery, onion, garlic, thyme, 1 teaspoon salt, and ¼ teaspoon pepper and continue to cook until the vegetables have a little color and are slightly tender—about 15 minutes (if anything starts to get too brown, add the chicken stock from the next step early).

3 Add the chicken stock to the pot with the veggies and bring the soup to a boil. Reduce it to a simmer and cook uncovered until the vegetables are very tender, but not mushy—15 to 20 minutes.

4 Remove two ladles (about 2 cups) of the veggies along with some stock from the pot and transfer to a blender; puree this mixture until it is very smooth. Transfer the puree back to the pot along with the chicken and stir to combine. Allow the soup to cook until the chicken is warmed through—3 to 5 minutes. Taste and add more salt if needed; this will depend on how salty your stock is.

5 Divide the egg noodles among serving bowls, then top with the chicken soup (I like to keep the

soup and noodles separate for leftovers—so the noodles don't become soggy). Garnish with additional thyme and black pepper and enjoy!

NOTE
Look for the delicious and nutritious high-quality bone broths that are sold in the freezer section. You can also add good-quality bouillon to regular boxed stock for a flavor bump.

zucchini + beans

grilled cheese with
sweet potato
(page 66)

tomato soup with basil yogurt drizzle

While tomato soup already has a lot of tomatoes (#Obvi), I thought I could make it into a real powerhouse dish. I decided to invite zucchini and cannellini beans over for lunch. Zucchini's bright summer flavor brings a subtle background note to the tomatoes, and the beans add a creamy finish without adding a bean taste. Altogether, this soup has a super classic flavor while delivering a modern nutritional punch.

MAKES 8 CUPS SOUP + 1½ CUPS DRIZZLE; SERVES 4

BASIL YOGURT DRIZZLE

1 cup plain Greek yogurt (8 ounces)
1 cup fresh basil leaves
½ teaspoon kosher salt

TOMATO SOUP WITH ZUCCHINI + BEANS

4 tablespoons unsalted butter
2 medium **zucchini** (14 ounces), chopped (3 cups)
1 medium yellow **onion** (8 ounces), chopped (1½ cups)
4 garlic cloves, minced
Kosher salt
One 15-ounce can **cannellini beans**, drained + rinsed
Two 14-ounce cans diced **tomatoes**
One 32-ounce can **tomato juice**
Ground black pepper
1 cup heavy cream
Fresh basil leaves, for a garnish

TO MAKE THE DRIZZLE:

Blend the yogurt, basil, and salt in a blender or food processor along with ½ cup water until the mixture is mostly smooth. If your blender has an extra-large base, you may need to use the food processor for this.

TO MAKE THE SOUP:

1 Melt the butter in a large pot over medium heat. Add the zucchini, onion, garlic, and 1 teaspoon salt, and cook until the vegetables are tender and fragrant—5 to 7 minutes.

2 Add the cooked veggies to a blender along with the cannellini beans and diced tomatoes; puree until very smooth. Return the mixture to the pot and add the tomato juice, another 1 teaspoon salt, and ¼ teaspoon pepper. Bring the mixture to a simmer and cook until slightly thickened— about 10 minutes. Add the cream to the pot and stir to combine.

3 To serve, divide the soup into bowls and top with the Basil Yogurt Drizzle, some basil leaves, and some pepper.

FREEZE IT
Freeze for up to 5 months. Thaw on the stovetop with a splash of water.

NOTE
If you have extra drizzle, use it as a topping for my Penne alla Vodka (page 119) or as a sauce for my Ultimate Veggie Burgers (page 145).

grilled cheese with sweet potato

My twins *love* cheese—they obviously take after their mama. While I was perfecting this recipe, I threw every veggie you could think of at a grilled cheese, and sweet potato was by far our favorite. Its slightly sweet taste and creamy-but-hearty texture offer up a perfect new pairing for that gooey cheese.

— MAKES 2 SANDWICHES —

1 small **sweet potato** (5 ounces)

1 cup shredded cheddar cheese (4 ounces)

4 slices bread

Mayonnaise or softened butter

1 Poke several holes in the sweet potato with a fork. Cook the sweet potato in the microwave on high for 2 minutes, then turn it over and microwave again until soft—about 2 minutes more.

2 Cut the sweet potato in half and scoop its flesh into a medium bowl. Using a potato masher or fork, mash the potato until it is smooth with no chunks remaining. This should give you about ¼ cup mashed sweet potato. Add the cheddar and stir to combine.

3 Spread half of the sweet potato mixture onto each of 2 slices of the bread, then top with the remaining 2 slices of bread, creating two sandwiches. Spread the mayonnaise or softened butter evenly to coat the sides of the bread facing out.

4 Heat a lidded skillet over medium heat, then place the sandwiches in the skillet and cook, covered, until the cheese is melted and the bread is golden brown—3 to 4 minutes a side. Serve hot.

SERVING SUGGESTION

Enjoy with my Tomato Soup with Basil Yogurt Drizzle (page 65) for a classic and irresistible combo.

NOTE

To make this with sliced cheese, spread 1 tablespoon sweet potato puree on each slice of bread, then layer on 2 to 3 slices of cheese per sandwich. The cheese and sweet potato will look more layered and not completely uniform, but it's still a delicious sandwich. Got leftover sweet potato? Freeze it for next time, or use it up in my Sweet Potato Tortillas (page 88) or Sweet Potato Pierogies (page 149).

SWAP IT

I like sweet potato the best, but other veggies like carrot, butternut squash, and cauliflower also work Just use ¼ cup puree for every 1 cup cheese.

roasted garlic, spinach + tomato grilled cheese

There's just nothing like a ripe tomato straight from the garden. The ones at the store are bred for shipping and color and are rarely vine ripened, so they don't have that garden-grown taste. Great news: roasting them transforms even lackluster tomatoes into all-star players. Pair them with some spinach, roasted garlic, and Parm and you've got a classic sandwich elevated to *OMG* status.

— MAKES 4 SANDWICHES —

3 medium **tomatoes**, sliced ½ inch thick (15 slices)

½ teaspoon Italian seasoning

Kosher salt

Ground black pepper

1 whole head of garlic

1 tablespoon olive oil

2 cups shredded mozzarella cheese (8 ounces)

2 cups **baby spinach** (2 ounces)

¼ cup grated Parmesan cheese (1 ounce) + more for sprinkling

Mayonnaise or softened butter

8 slices sourdough bread

1 Preheat the oven to 400°F. Line a baking sheet with parchment paper. Place the tomato slices on the prepared baking sheet, then sprinkle them with the Italian seasoning, ¼ teaspoon salt, and a pinch of pepper.

2 Cut off and discard the top third of the garlic bulb (the nonroot end), exposing all the cloves in the remainder; place the remainder cut-side-up on a square of aluminum foil. Drizzle the oil over the cut surface. Wrap the foil around the garlic, making sure it doesn't touch the cut surface, and seal tightly. Place on the baking sheet with the tomato slices. Roast until the garlic is lightly browned and tender and the tomatoes have shrunken and are charred in spots—about 40 minutes.

3 When the garlic is cool enough to handle, squeeze the whole head of garlic to pop the cloves out of their skins and into the bowl of a food processor. Add the mozzarella, spinach, Parmesan, and another ¼ teaspoon salt. Pulse until the ingredients are finely chopped and well combined.

4 Spread the mayonnaise or butter on one side of each slice of bread. Place 4 slices of the bread on a work surface with the mayo or butter side down, and top each with a heaping ½ cup spinach-cheese mixture, 3 to 4 tomato slices, and a sprinkle of Parmesan. Place the remaining 4 slices of bread on top, mayo side up.

5 Heat a large lidded skillet over medium heat. Working in batches if necessary, cook the sandwiches, covered, until the cheese is melted and the bread is golden brown on both sides—2 to 3 minutes per side. Cut and serve.

cauliflower egg salad sandwiches

My mom always said, "If you've got eggs, you've got a meal!" and I totally subscribe to that idea. With eggs you can easily make egg salad, which is for sure a meal, and a great one at that. But to make this even more of a complete meal, let's bring browned cauliflower on board—its subtle nuttiness makes you wonder why it wasn't always part of your recipe. To change things up, you can use pre-riced cauliflower for subtle texture or finely chopped cauliflower for a tender-crisp bite that mimics and complements the crunch of that celery. Either way, we've got eggs *and* veggies. I don't know if I've ever made my mom so proud.

———————— MAKES 1 OR 2 SANDWICHES (WITH 2 CUPS EGG SALAD) ————————

4 large eggs

Kosher salt

1 teaspoon olive oil

½ cup riced or finely chopped **cauliflower** (1½ ounces)

¼ cup mayonnaise

¼ cup finely chopped celery

1 tablespoon finely chopped scallions

2 teaspoons Dijon mustard

¼ teaspoon paprika

4 slices bread, toasted if desired

Lettuce leaves

1 Begin by hard-boiling the eggs. In a small saucepan, cover them by about 1 inch with cold water; to make the eggs easier to peel, add a large pinch of salt to the water. Bring the water to a boil, then cover the pan and remove it from the heat. Allow the eggs to sit for 12 minutes (set a timer because if you're anything like me, it's almost guaranteed you'll forget). Transfer the eggs to a bowl of ice water to cool and set them aside.

2 While the eggs boil, heat the oil in a small sauté pan over medium-high heat. Add the cauliflower and a small pinch of salt and cook, stirring frequently, until the cauliflower is tender and browned—3 to 5 minutes. Remove the pan from the heat.

3 Peel the cooled eggs and chop them into ½-inch pieces. In a large bowl, gently toss the eggs, cauliflower, mayonnaise, celery, scallions, mustard, paprika, and ¼ teaspoon salt until they are well combined.

4 Place some of the lettuce leaves onto 2 slices of the bread, then divide the egg salad between them. Top with additional lettuce, then the remaining slices of bread to form two sandwiches. Or make one awesome club-style sandwich with 3 slices of bread and all the egg salad. You're an adult—you don't need to share!

cauliflower

cauliflower crust lunch box pizzas

I call these "lunch box pizzas" because they're the perfect size to fit in lunch boxes—with room for some sides and maybe even a veggie-fied sweet treat. And because you've got so much to do besides packing lunches, I'm keeping this simple—the dough is made in the food processor, you don't have to precook the cauliflower, and there is no yeast, so no rise time. Once the pizzas are made, wrap them individually and put them in the fridge or freezer, then pull them out one at a time as needed. Easy, make-ahead, and everyone is eating cauliflower!

—— MAKES TWELVE 4-INCH MINI PIZZAS ——

1½ cups **cauliflower rice**, fresh or thawed from frozen (4½ ounces)

¾ cup plain Greek yogurt (6 ounces)

¼ cup grated Parmesan cheese (1 ounce)

1 teaspoon baking powder

1 teaspoon kosher salt

1 teaspoon garlic powder

2 cups all-purpose flour

¾ cup pizza sauce

1½ cups shredded mozzarella cheese (6 ounces)

Mini pepperoni (optional)

1 Preheat the oven to 400°F. Spray two baking sheets with cooking oil spray. Puree the cauliflower rice, yogurt, Parmesan, baking powder, salt, and garlic powder in a food processor until the mixture is well combined and mostly smooth. Add the flour and process again until a dough forms. If your food processor has any trouble with the mixture, simply remove it and work it together by hand; if the dough is too dry and is not coming together, add 1 tablespoon more of yogurt or water.

2 On a heavily floured surface, shape the dough into a ball and divide it equally into twelve pieces; I like to do this by cutting the dough into four quarters, then cutting each of the quarters into three equal pieces. Form the dough pieces into balls, then flatten them into 4-inch rounds using your hands or a rolling pin.

3 Divide the rounds between the two prepared baking sheets, then spray the tops of them with cooking oil spray or brush them with olive oil. Bake until the bottom sides of the rounds are lightly browned—about 8 minutes—then flip and continue baking until the tops are also lightly browned and the crusts are cooked through—5 to 8 minutes more.

4 Remove from the oven and set the broiler to high. Top each pizza crust with about 1 tablespoon sauce, 2 tablespoons mozzarella, and a couple of mini pepperonis (if desired). Broil the pizzas until the cheese is melted and the crusts are nicely browned—about 2 minutes.

5 Serve fresh and hot, or allow the pizzas to cool, wrap them individually in foil, and put them in the fridge for easy lunch box entrées.

FREEZE IT

Freeze the cooked pizzas once they are completely cooled. When you're ready to eat, remove them from the freezer, transfer them to a baking sheet or place directly onto the oven rack, then bake at 350°F for 10 to 12 minutes.

chicken nuggets

What if a nugget could be more than just a hunk of protein, something closer to a complete meal? Sounds incredible, doesn't it? Well, this was my #MomDream, and after putting in lots of time in a nugget-filled kitchen, I can now proudly say that it's a reality.

These nuggets have as much beans and carrots in them as they do chicken, giving you something you just can't find at the store. They go fast around here, so I tend to make extra and freeze them, or even form them into patties for chicken burgers.

MAKES 25 NUGGETS

2 medium **carrots** (5 ounces), chopped (1 cup)

One 15-ounce can **cannellini beans**, drained + rinsed

½ cup grated Parmesan cheese (2 ounces)

¼ cup mayonnaise

3 chicken bouillon cubes or 1 tablespoon chicken bouillon base

1 teaspoon garlic powder

1 teaspoon onion powder

½ teaspoon kosher salt

½ cup + ½ cup Italian breadcrumbs, divided + more as needed

1 pound ground chicken

2 tablespoons olive oil + more if needed

1 Process the carrots in a food processor until they are very finely chopped. Add the cannellini beans, Parmesan, mayonnaise, bouillon cubes or bouillon base, garlic powder, onion powder, and salt, and blend until everything comes together and you can no longer see pieces of beans. Add ½ cup of the breadcrumbs and pulse a couple of times until everything is combined.

2 Transfer the bean mixture to a large bowl, add the chicken, and mix until just combined (try not to overmix)—your hands work best here.

3 Place the remaining ½ cup breadcrumbs in a bowl or plate. Scoop about ¼ cup of the chicken mixture into your hand, roll it into a ball, then smash it flat into the breadcrumbs; flip it to coat all sides with the breadcrumbs, then form it into an oval and add dents here and there along the sides to mimic the shape of a store-bought nugget. The chicken mixture will be a little soft and that's okay, but if you are having a lot of trouble forming your nuggets, you can always throw your mixture in the fridge (it will firm up as it cools down) or add a few more breadcrumbs to the chicken mixture to help it hold together.

4 Heat the oil in a large skillet over medium heat. Working in batches, add the nuggets to the skillet and cook them until both sides of the nuggets are golden brown and the nuggets are firm and cooked through—4 to 6 minutes per side. Repeat this process until all the nuggets have been cooked, adding more oil as needed. The easiest way to tell if the nuggets are done is to use a thermometer; you want to see their internal temperatures reach 165°F. Alternatively,

spray the nuggets with cooking oil spray and bake
at 425°F for 15 to 20 minutes.

STORE IT + FREEZE IT

*Once the nuggets are totally cooled, store
them in the refrigerator for up to a week
or freeze for up to 3 months. From
frozen, reheat the nuggets by baking at
375°F for 8 to 10 minutes.*

SWAP IT

*Replace the cannellini beans with other
white beans like navy beans or great
northern beans. And swap the mayo
for whole-milk Greek yogurt if
you prefer.*

raspberry beet vinaigrette

For whatever reason, my kids have always been fascinated with salads. And a pink dressing makes them—and me!—extra excited. Although I'm not the biggest beet fan, it's amazing how many beets you can add here without overpowering those sweet raspberries; the beets balance out and enhance the raspberry flavor with a slight earthiness. Overall, the result of this fruit + veggie mash-up gives you a tasty and colorful vinaigrette perfect for kids and parents alike.

— MAKES 2¼ CUPS —

1 medium **beet** (5 ounces),
  roasted + peeled
1¼ cups raspberries
  (6 ounces), fresh or frozen
½ cup apple cider vinegar
¼ cup honey
1 tablespoon Dijon mustard
1 teaspoon kosher salt
Juice + zest of 1 lemon
1 cup olive oil

Blend the beet, raspberries, apple cider vinegar, honey, mustard, salt, lemon juice, and lemon zest in a blender until smooth. Leave the blender on and slowly drizzle in the oil, starting with a couple of drops and slowly adding more until it is all incorporated and the dressing thickens. Add to your favorite salad and enjoy!

STORE IT

Leftover dressing can be stored in an airtight container in the refrigerator for up to 2 weeks.

No one loves a picnic
as much as Ivy.

ham + cheese wraps in homemade spinach tortillas

Wraps are the object of almost everyone's food crushes—they're light yet filling, crunchy and customizable, and really there is never a bad time to devour one. And when you start making your own fresh, no-yeast spinach tortillas, which are soft and slightly chewy with a hit of salty cheddar, your innocent infatuation will officially become romance novel material. Add some smoky ham and tangy provolone and get ready for *50 Shades of Green* to premiere in a kitchen near you.

—— MAKES 4 WRAPS (PLUS 8 EXTRA TORTILLAS!) ——

SPINACH TORTILLAS

5 cups **baby spinach** (5 ounces)

1 cup shredded cheddar cheese (4 ounces)

2 teaspoons baking powder

2 teaspoons kosher salt

3 cups all-purpose flour + more as needed

WRAPS

4 tablespoons mayonnaise

4 teaspoons Dijon mustard

12 slices deli ham

8 slices provolone cheese

Lettuce

1 tomato, sliced

TO MAKE THE TORTILLAS:

1 Process the spinach along with ½ cup water in a food processor until the mixture is pureed, scraping down the sides of the bowl as needed. Add the cheddar, baking powder, and salt and process again until all the ingredients are well combined. Add the flour and process once more until a dough forms. If the dough is too wet and/or sticky, add a touch more flour. If it's crumbly and won't come together easily when you squeeze it in your hands, add a splash of water.

2 Transfer the dough to a floured surface and knead it a couple of times to form a ball. Divide it into eight equal pieces (cut it like a pizza), then roll each piece out until it is 9 to 10 inches in diameter and slightly thinner than ⅛ inch thick (the thinner the better).

CONTINUED . . .

. . . CONTINUED

3 Place a piece of aluminum foil (about 10 × 15 inches) on a counter or tabletop. Heat a large cast-iron or high-heat nonstick skillet over high heat until the pan is very hot. Place one of the tortillas in the skillet (no oil is necessary) and cook until the underside has brown spots and the tortilla starts to bubble up—30 seconds to 1 minute. Flip the tortilla and cook until it is dry all over and some brown spots have appeared on the side now facing the pan—30 seconds to 1 minute more.

4 When the tortilla is cooked, place it on one side of the large piece of foil and fold the unused portion of the foil over so that the tortilla is covered for the time being. (Do not skip this step. This is not just to keep the tortillas warm; the tortillas will gently steam one another as you add more, which is the key to making tortillas that are supple and will not

crack.) Repeat this process with the remaining tortillas, lifting the folded foil piece to add finished tortillas to the stack, then refolding the foil over the stack to retain the heat. When you are finished cooking all the tortillas, tightly seal up the foil around the stack and allow them to sit in the foil for 10 minutes to continue steaming.

TO MAKE THE WRAPS:

1 Spread 1 tablespoon mayo and 1 teaspoon mustard on each of the 4 Spinach Tortillas, then layer each with 3 slices of ham and 2 slices of provolone, covering the surface of the tortilla. Divide the lettuce and tomato slices evenly among the 4 tortillas, placing the veggies off to one side of each tortilla.

2 To assemble, begin rolling the wrap on the veggie side of the tortilla. Roll tightly, secure with toothpicks, and serve.

STORE IT + FREEZE IT

The tortillas last in the fridge for up to a week. When you're ready to use, warm them in the microwave for 15 seconds or wrap them in foil and warm in a 350°F oven for 1 to 2 minutes. Freeze tortillas for up to 5 months; thaw by microwaving for 20 to 30 seconds or wrapping in foil and baking at 350°F for 2 minutes.

eggplant chicken tenders

Why bread chicken using eggs when you can use egg*plant*? And why use any old coating when you can mix together cereal and wheat germ for serious crunch and fiber? Oh, and why make just "okay" chicken tenders when you can make *insanely good* ones—as in, your plate of tenders is suddenly empty and you're already devising a plan to steal one from your kids' quickly dwindling stash? The answer to all these "whys" is simply "why *not*?"

——————————— MAKES 12 TO 15 CHICKEN TENDERS ———————————

1 medium **eggplant** (1 pound)

1 tablespoon olive oil

Kosher salt

Ground black pepper

5 cups corn or wheat flake cereal (9 ounces), such as cornflakes

⅓ cup **wheat germ**

1 teaspoon garlic powder

1 teaspoon onion powder

12–15 chicken tenders (2 pounds)

¾ cup all-purpose flour

Canola or avocado oil, for frying

1 Preheat the oven to 425°F. Cut the eggplant in half lengthwise and place the halves cut-side-up on a rimmed baking sheet. Drizzle them lightly with the olive oil, then sprinkle with ½ teaspoon salt and ¼ teaspoon pepper. Bake the eggplant until it is very soft—about 30 minutes. Remove the eggplant from the oven and set it aside to cool slightly.

2 While the eggplant cooks, pulse the cereal several times in a food processor until it is coarsely chopped and looks similar to large panko breadcrumbs. Add the wheat germ, garlic powder, onion powder, ½ teaspoon salt, and ¼ teaspoon pepper to the food processor and pulse just a couple of times to mix everything together. Transfer the cereal coating to a medium bowl (no need to clean out the food processor— you'll need it in the next step), then set aside.

3 When the eggplant is cool enough to handle, use a spoon to scrape its flesh into the food processor; discard the skin and stem. Process until the eggplant is completely pureed (this should give you about 1 cup puree), then transfer it to a second medium bowl.

4 Season the chicken tenders on all sides using another ½ teaspoon salt and ¼ teaspoon pepper. Add the flour to a third medium bowl. Toss each tender, one at a time, in the flour, coating it completely, then shaking off any excess. Transfer the chicken to the bowl with the eggplant, again coating it completely (a pastry brush can really help to evenly coat). Next, transfer the tender to the bowl with the cereal, making sure to get a good coating of the cereal on all sides of the chicken tender by really pressing the cereal into it.

TO FRY: Fill a large high-sided skillet with ¼ to ½ inch of oil, then heat it over medium-high heat until it begins to shimmer.

Carefully dip the tip of one of the breaded chicken tenders in the hot oil; if the oil bubbles vigorously, it is ready; if not, wait another minute and try again (your oil should be about 375°F). When the oil is hot, working in batches of four (you don't want to crowd the pan), fry the tenders in the oil until they are golden brown and cooked through (165°F)—3 to 4 minutes per side. Continue frying until all the chicken tenders are done, transferring cooked tenders to a cooling rack to help them stay crispy while you finish up.

TO BAKE: Spray a baking sheet with cooking oil spray. Place the breaded tenders on the prepared baking sheet, and then drizzle them with olive oil or spray them with cooking oil spray. Bake at 400°F for 10 minutes, then flip and continue cooking until they are lightly browned and cooked through—another 7 to 10 minutes. An air fryer also works great.

FREEZE IT

Freeze cooked and cooled chicken tenders for up to 3 months. To thaw, bake at 400°F, flipping halfway through the cooking time, until the breading is crispy and the chicken is heated through—15 to 20 minutes.

yellow squash

yellow squash corn tortillas

I like recipes that work every time and include ingredients that are easily sourced. Traditionally, corn tortillas are made with masa harina, a unique type of very finely ground Mexican corn flour. It's a specialty ingredient that I've gotten my hands on once or twice, but it's not exactly a supermarket staple everywhere.

However, I *do* always have cornmeal on hand. Although cornmeal has a great flavor, the texture is pretty coarse, so mixing cornmeal and flour together mellows it out, giving you a taste and texture similar to masa harina's. Oh! And did I mention the yellow squash? The pureed squash moistens the dough to perfection, plumping up the flour and cornmeal and bringing it all together. My kids are obsessed with these—we use them for quesadillas or beef tacos, or cook them up into chips (see my note below).

―――――――――――― MAKES TEN 6-INCH TORTILLAS ――――――――――――

1 small **yellow squash** (6 ounces), chopped (1½ cups)

1¾ cups all-purpose flour

1 cup yellow cornmeal

6 tablespoons canola or avocado oil

1½ teaspoons kosher salt

1 teaspoon garlic powder

1 **FOOD PROCESSOR:** Process the yellow squash and ¼ cup water, blending until the mixture is smooth. This should give you ¾ cup squash puree (it's important to be exact, so measure it out in a measuring cup). If you find you have less than ¾ cup puree, add more water to reach ¾ cup, and if you end up with more, put the extra aside in case you need it later on. Add the flour, cornmeal, oil, salt, and garlic powder to the food processor along with the squash puree and process until a dough forms, clumping together and pulling away from the sides of the bowl. You may need to use a spatula to move it around and scrape down the bowl halfway through processing. If your dough is too dry to come together, add 2 tablespoons more of your leftover squash puree or 2 tablespoons water.

BLENDER + BY HAND: Blend the squash and ½ cup water, processing until the mixture is very smooth, then measure out ¾ cup squash puree (it's important to be exact) and transfer it to a large bowl; reserve any extra squash puree in case you need it. Add the flour, cornmeal, oil, salt, and garlic powder to the bowl and mix until a moist dough forms. Once the dough has mostly come together, knead it on your countertop until it is nice and smooth—1 to 2 minutes. If your dough is too dry to come together, add 2 tablespoons more of the squash puree or 2 tablespoons water.

CONTINUED . . .

2 Using your hands, roll about ¼ cup of the dough into a ball. On a lightly floured surface, roll the ball out into a very thin circle, just a little thicker than paper thin; it will thicken as it cooks, so make it thinner than you want your final product to be. Place the rolled-out tortillas on a lightly floured baking sheet and continue until you have formed all of the dough into rounds.

3 Heat a large cast-iron or high-heat nonstick skillet over high heat. Place a large piece of aluminum foil (about 10 × 15 inches) on a counter or tabletop. Make sure the pan is very hot, then cook one of the dough rounds in the dry pan (no oil is necessary) until multiple bubbles form on top and the underside has brown spots—30 to 45 seconds. Flip and cook the tortilla until just a couple of brown spots form on the side now facing the pan—10 to 15 seconds more. You don't want the tortilla to be in the pan for too long or it will dry out and break; hot and fast is what we're looking for. When the tortilla is ready, it should not be completely dried out; you should see both brown spots and moist spots on its surface.

4 As you finish cooking each tortilla, place it on one side of the large piece of foil and fold the unused portion of the foil over so that the tortilla is covered for the time being. (Do not skip this step. This is not just to keep the tortillas warm; the tortillas will gently steam one another as you add more, which is the key to making tortillas that are supple and will not crack.) Repeat this process with the remaining tortillas, lifting the folded foil piece to add finished tortillas to the stack, then refolding the foil over the stack to retain the heat. When you are finished cooking all the tortillas, tightly seal up the foil around the stack and allow them to sit in the foil for at least 10 minutes, but ideally 30 minutes (even 30 minutes later they will still be warm).

SERVING SUGGESTIONS

Fill the warm tortillas with my Taco Meat with Pinto Beans (page 100) or load them up with scrambled eggs + salsa or bacon + lettuce + tomato.

NOTES

* Make these into chips! After cooking the tortillas, cut each one into six triangles. Spray a baking sheet with cooking oil spray and add the triangles in a single layer. Spray the triangles with cooking oil spray and sprinkle them with salt. Bake at 300°F until they are slightly brown and crispy—20 to 25 minutes; these will continue to crisp up as they cool.

* For a subtle zing, add the zest from 1 lime to the tortilla dough before rolling—kind of like a lime tortilla chip.

STORE IT

Store tortillas in the fridge for up to a week. To reheat, wrap them completely in foil and bake at 350°F for 5 to 15 minutes, depending on how many tortillas you have. If you are reheating a bunch, open the foil package and move the ones from the middle to the outside halfway through cooking for even warming. Note that these do not warm well in the microwave as they start to dry out and break.

sweet potato tortillas

Rarely a week goes by when you will not find sweet potato tortillas in my fridge. I find myself making them so consistently because, yes, they are incredibly delicious, but also because I always have the ingredients on hand—they're just sweet potatoes, flour, salt, and garlic powder. The sweet potatoes give the tortillas a touch of sweetness and an irresistibly chewy quality while being stable enough to fill with anything you can think of. So get ready for egg + cheese tacos in the morning, turkey + tomato wraps for lunch, and pepper jack quesadillas for a late-night snack.

— MAKES SIX 6-INCH TORTILLAS —

1 large **sweet potato** (10 ounces)

1 cup all-purpose flour + more as needed

1 teaspoon kosher salt

½ teaspoon garlic powder

1 Poke several holes in the sweet potato with a fork. Cook the sweet potato in the microwave on high until soft—4 to 5 minutes.

2 **BY HAND:** When the sweet potato is cool enough to handle, peel off and discard the skin and place the flesh in a medium bowl. Mash the peeled sweet potato with a fork or potato masher, then add the flour along with the salt and garlic powder. Mix together until a dough forms, adding more flour as necessary. Knead the dough on a heavily floured work surface until the flour is completely incorporated and the dough is tacky but not super sticky, adding more flour as needed.

FOOD PROCESSOR + MIXER: Remove and discard the skin of the sweet potato, place the flesh in the bowl of a food processor or stand mixer, and process/beat until it is nearly smooth. Add the flour, salt, and garlic powder and process/mix again until the dough forms, adding more flour as necessary until it is rollable and tacky but not super sticky.

3 Divide the dough into six equal pieces and roll each into a ball; on a heavily floured surface, roll each ball into a 6-inch round, about ¹⁄₁₆ inch thick, brushing the excess flour from each tortilla.

4 Heat a large cast-iron or high-heat nonstick skillet over high heat, make sure it's very hot, and add one of the tortillas (no oil is necessary). Cook until the underside has brown spots and the tortilla starts to puff up—about

2 minutes. Flip the tortilla and cook until brown spots appear on the side now facing the pan—1 to 2 minutes more. Repeat with the remaining tortillas. Serve warm with your favorite fillings.

STORE IT + FREEZE IT

Tortillas are good in the fridge for up to a week; just be sure to warm them slightly in the oven or microwave before using. You can also freeze these for up to 5 months; to thaw, bake at 350°F for 2 minutes or microwave on high for 15 to 30 seconds.

NOTE

Make these into chips! Cut into triangles and spray with cooking oil spray; bake at 325°F until they are slightly brown and crispy—15 to 18 minutes; these will continue to crisp up as they cool. These chips will be thicker than tortilla chips, more like pita chips.

strawberry + chia jam

Talk about easy! Some strawberries, a little sugar, some lemon, and chia seeds to thicken things up, and 15 minutes later you've got jam. Chia seeds can be added to things raw for a nice little crunch, but when cooked or left to soak, they swell up, absorbing more than 10 times their weight in water, thickening whatever you put them in—they will absorb any excess water in your jam, giving it a perfect consistency. Besides making for a foolproof jam, chia seeds are super high in fiber, antioxidants, protein, iron, and calcium, which is why they're a favorite ingredient in my house.

MAKES 1 CUP

2 cups stemmed strawberries, fresh or frozen (10 ounces)

Kosher salt

¼ cup granulated sugar + more to taste

2 tablespoons chia seeds

Juice of 1 lemon (2 tablespoons; optional)

1 If your fresh strawberries are extra-large, cut them in half (keep frozen ones whole, even if large). In a small saucepan over medium heat, cook the strawberries along with 2 tablespoons water and a pinch of salt, stirring to combine. Bring this mixture to a simmer and cook, stirring frequently, until the strawberries have broken down and most of the water has evaporated—15 to 20 minutes.

2 Turn the heat to low and use a potato masher or fork to mash the strawberry mixture until it is mostly smooth. For a completely smooth jam, blend the strawberry mixture in a food processor or blender until smooth, then transfer back to the pan over low heat.

3 Stir in the sugar, chia seeds, and lemon juice if desired and cook until the ingredients are well incorporated and the sugar is fully dissolved—2 to 3 minutes. Carefully taste the jam (it's hot!) and see if it needs more sugar. The recipe calls for a low amount of sugar in comparison to other jam recipes, and sometimes I do need to add an extra 1 to 2 tablespoons, depending on how sweet the fruit was to begin with.

4 Transfer the jam to a jar and allow it to cool completely before serving. It will thicken as it

cools and the chia seeds will work their magic, so don't worry if it looks a little thin.

RASPBERRY JAM

Sub in 2 cups raspberries, fresh or frozen (8 to 10 ounces), for the strawberries, and reduce the cook time to 5 minutes in Step 1. Raspberries break down very easily, so you'll get a perfectly smooth jam with no blender or mashing required. Raspberries are actually my favorite, but you can also try blackberries, blueberries, or mixed berries. These should take 10 to 20 minutes to cook.

STORE IT + FREEZE IT

Store in the fridge for up to 4 weeks or freeze for up to 1 year. To thaw from frozen, put jam in the fridge overnight.

peanut butter + hummus spread

I promise it tastes just like peanut butter! Although combining peanut butter and hummus might not have been your first thought, they really do go well together. And I love that my kids (especially the hummus hater, Ivy) are getting some chickpeas in their PB+J. It's not a ton of chickpeas per sandwich, but I always feel like a lot of little wins eventually add up.

———— MAKES ENOUGH PEANUT BUTTER FOR 2 PB+JS ————

2 tablespoons peanut butter
1 tablespoon plain hummus

In a small bowl, stir the peanut butter and hummus until they are well combined and the mixture is smooth. I find this works best with unrefrigerated peanut butter, as it's easier to mix and spread. Spread on a slice of bread or enjoy on some celery or as part of your PB+J.

NOTE

When making PB+J, I often just mix the peanut butter and hummus directly on the bread with my knife; as long as you have two parts peanut butter to one part hummus, you're good to go.

strawberry + beet jam

It may shock you to know that I don't love every veggie. There are still some I'm learning to love—like beets. I know, though, that subtle exposure to them over time is a surefire way to get that love affair started. So let's do it!

There is definitely some beet flavor in this jam, but here it adds earthiness and depth of flavor to the brightness of the sweet strawberries. It makes for a more sophisticated jam, while still being totally strawberry-forward. And the kids—and even I—love it.

— MAKES 2 CUPS —

3 cups stemmed strawberries, fresh or frozen (16 ounces)

1 medium **beet** (5 ounces), roasted, peeled, and chopped (1 cup), or one 8.25-ounce can sliced or whole **beets**, drained + rinsed

Kosher salt

¾ cup granulated sugar + more to taste

3 tablespoons **chia seeds**

Juice of 1 lemon (2 tablespoons)

STORE IT + FREEZE IT

Store in the fridge for up to 4 weeks or freeze for up to 1 year. To thaw, refrigerate frozen jam overnight.

NOTE

Still working on that love affair with beets? Start with a flavor closer to a traditional strawberry jam by using just 1 small beet in this recipe.

1 If your fresh strawberries are extra-large, cut them in half (keep frozen ones whole even if large). Heat the strawberries in a medium saucepan over medium heat along with the beets, 2 tablespoons water, and a pinch of salt, stirring to combine. Bring this mixture to a simmer and cook, stirring frequently, until the strawberries have broken down completely and most of the water has evaporated but the mixture is not completely thick—15 to 20 minutes.

2 Carefully transfer the hot berries and beets to a blender and blend until the mixture is smooth.

3 Return the mixture to the pot. Stir in the sugar, chia seeds, and lemon juice, and cook over low heat until they are well incorporated and the sugar is fully dissolved—1 to 2 minutes. Carefully taste the jam and see if it needs more sugar; sometimes I add an extra 1 to 2 tablespoons, depending on how sweet the fruit was to begin with.

4 Transfer the jam to a large jar (or you could transfer it to two small jars and freeze one of them). The chia seeds will work their magic, and the jam will thicken as it cools, so don't worry if it looks a little thin. Cool completely before serving or freezing.

MORE VEGGIES AT DINNER

If breakfast is a fail, eh, whatever. The lunch box comes back still loaded with cucumbers and peppers? Hmm, but no huge deal. But there is something about dinner that feels big—it has to go well.

And there is literally nothing worse than preparing a big, made-from-scratch dinner only to have everyone take one bite and stop eating. You feel defeated and start to wonder why you didn't just thaw some fish sticks and French fries. Well, have no fear, I have worked tirelessly to make classic dinner dishes like mac and cheese, pizza, and burgers into veggie-fied versions everyone will love. You'll be handing out smiles and veggies at your dinner table tonight.

cauliflower +
sweet potato

mac + cheese with cauliflower + sweet potato

This is the most important recipe in the book. Not only because mac and cheese is an iconic American dish (and my personal favorite), but because this recipe shows you the thought process that goes into every dish found in these pages. Like all my recipes, this version of the classic is loaded with veggies, but that's a secondary thing. First and foremost, it's just plain *good*—like taking-bite-after-bite-until-you-realize-you've-licked-the-bowl-clean *good*.

I don't want to have to sell you on my food by telling you it's packed with veggies. This mac and cheese, for instance, should just be the best mac and cheese you've ever eaten. Period. And the added bonus is that when you're finished, you'll remember, oh yeah, it's made with 6 cups of veggies! Delicious *and* nutritious.

--- SERVES 8 ---

1–2 pounds elbow macaroni (see note)

1 tablespoon + 4 tablespoons unsalted butter, divided

1 small yellow **onion** (5 ounces), chopped (1 cup)

3 garlic cloves, sliced

½ small head **cauliflower** (9 ounces), chopped (3 cups)

1 medium **sweet potato** (8 ounces), peeled + chopped (2 cups)

Kosher salt

½ + 2 cups whole milk, divided + more as needed

¼ cup all-purpose flour

1 teaspoon mustard powder

1 teaspoon garlic powder

2 cups shredded cheddar cheese (8 ounces)

6 slices American cheese (4 ounces)

1 cup grated Parmesan cheese (4 ounces)

Ground black pepper (optional)

1 Place a large pot of salted water over high heat for cooking the macaroni. When the water boils, add the macaroni and cook according to the package directions. Drain. If not using right away, add a splash of olive oil and stir well so that the macaroni doesn't stick together as it sits; set aside.

2 Meanwhile, heat 1 tablespoon of the butter in a large saucepan over medium heat. Add the onion and garlic and sauté until tender—about 5 minutes. Stir in the cauliflower, sweet potato, ½ cup water, and 1 teaspoon salt. Bring this mixture to a boil and then reduce to a simmer. Cook covered, stirring occasionally, until the vegetables are very tender and almost all the liquid has evaporated—about 15 minutes.

3 Transfer the veggie mixture to a blender along with ½ cup of the milk and let the blender run, processing the mixture until it is as smooth as possible; set aside. (If your blender can handle it, don't be afraid to let it run for 1 to 2 minutes for a super silky-smooth result.)

4 Melt the remaining 4 tablespoons butter in the empty veggie pot over medium heat. Once the butter is melted, add the flour and whisk until well combined. Cook for 2 minutes, whisking occasionally. Slowly add

CONTINUED . . .

step 2   step 3   step 4   step 5

. . . CONTINUED

the remaining 2 cups milk, whisking continuously as you pour; continue whisking until the mixture is smooth (a whisk is an important tool here—a spoon will not work well). Cook until the mixture boils and thickens—about 2 minutes. Then stir in the veggie puree along with the mustard powder, garlic powder, and another 1 teaspoon salt.

5 Turn the heat to low and stir in the cheddar, American, and Parmesan cheeses until melted. Taste the cheese sauce and add more salt if needed; this depends on the saltiness of your cheese (I often season with ½ teaspoon or more salt here; you have a lot of veggies in this pot and it takes a good amount of salt to make them sing). You can also add some pepper here if desired.

6 Add the cooked macaroni to the pot with the sauce and toss to combine. (If you are still unsure how cheesy you want your mac and cheese, scoop out half of the cheese sauce before adding the noodles. Taste and keep adding more cheese sauce until it's just how you like it.) If the mac and cheese seems too thick, or thickens after sitting on the stovetop, add a splash of water or milk to thin it out a bit and bring it back to life.

HACK IT

I know you want a Hack It note here, and a great one. But I have to be honest—adding some sort of veggie puree to a boxed mac never goes over well in my house. Or I use such a tiny amount of puree that I'm not sure it's worth it. If you really want to try, make sure you're using a boxed brand with a liquid cheese sauce (it hides the veggie puree better than powdered cheese brands) and add 1 tablespoon at a time of pureed sweet potato or cauliflower. Be careful not to add too much; kids don't like their favorite boxed mac messed with, and it will end up being your dinner. You know I've been there.

FREEZE IT

The sauce freezes great! I like to freeze just the sauce by itself, without the noodles. Freeze 1-cup portions and serve by adding 1 cup thawed sauce to ½ pound freshly cooked pasta. Save some of the pasta cooking water (or use regular water) and add to the pan with the frozen sauce when ready to thaw, it will help it thaw properly and really bring it back to life..

SWAP IT

If you prefer not to use American cheese, my favorite sub is 4 ounces of cream cheese, but you can also use 4 ounces of a melty cheese like Colby, Muenster, or Monterey Jack.

NOTE

Use 1 pound of pasta for a very cheesy mac, or you can easily stretch the meal with up to 2 pounds of pasta. I generally toss about half the sauce with 1 pound of pasta and freeze the remaining cheese sauce by itself for another meal.

baked mac + cheese

Toss 1½ pounds cooked pasta with all of the sauce, then pour into a 13 × 9-inch baking dish. Top with a mix of 1 cup panko breadcrumbs and 1 cup grated Parmesan cheese. Bake at 350°F until golden brown and crunchy on top—40 to 45 minutes.

taco meat with pinto beans

Tacos seem to be on everyone's weekly menu. So I knew I had to make basic taco meat much more than basic. By mashing pinto beans into the meat at just the right moment, I'm able to keep the texture and crunchy bits of the beef while seamlessly incorporating those beans—which means I'm adding fiber and protein, and I'm stretching the meat on your plate. Pair all this with warm-but-not-spicy seasonings and you've got your new Taco Tuesday classic. Or Monday, or Sunday . . . or all the days!

———————— MAKES ENOUGH FILLING FOR 6 LARGE OR 12 SMALL TACOS ————————

1½ teaspoons chili powder

1 teaspoon ground cumin

1 teaspoon paprika

Kosher salt

Ground black pepper

One 15-ounce can **pinto beans**, drained + rinsed

1 tablespoon olive oil

1 pound ground beef

3 tablespoons **tomato** paste

1 In a small bowl, stir together the chili powder, cumin, paprika, ½ teaspoon salt, and ¼ teaspoon pepper, then set aside. In a medium bowl, use a fork or potato masher to mash the pinto beans until they are mostly smooth.

2 Heat the oil in a large skillet over medium-high heat, then add the beef, spreading it as best you can into an even layer with your spoon. Season the beef with another ½ teaspoon salt and ¼ teaspoon pepper and allow it to cook undisturbed (don't touch it!) until it is deeply brown and crispy on the pan side—about 5 minutes.

3 Once the beef is nicely brown, spread the beans on top of it and push down on them with your spoon to mash them into the beef. Break up the beef up and flip it over to cook on the other side.

4 Add the seasoning mixture and tomato paste to the pan and stir until all ingredients are combined. Cook until the spices are fragrant and the meat is cooked through—about 5 minutes more. Serve and enjoy!

HACK IT

Usually use a taco seasoning packet? Why stop now? Follow the recipe as written, but omit the chili powder, ground cumin, paprika, salt, pepper, and tomato paste; cook up the meat and beans as described in Steps 2 and 3, then add your seasoning packet along with the packet's recommended amount of water. Stir and cook for 3 to 4 minutes more.

½ meat, ½ beans

mushrooms,
onions, celery,
carrot + tomatoes

mushroom + beef bolognese

Whenever I make Bolognese, I feel like I'm killing it at life. I'm tapping into my Italian roots and making a rich sauce that always seems to be able to stretch for as many people, and portions, as I want. The house smells like Italian heaven, where I imagine there is always a pot of sauce simmering. My kids all eat dinner, with no complaints—and even ask for seconds. And with this version of Bolognese, I know that they eat twice as many veggies (mushrooms, onions, celery, carrots, and tomatoes!) as beef. It's a Tuesday, the red wine is flowing, and life is good.

MAKES 5 CUPS; SERVES 6

2 tablespoons olive oil + more as needed

1 pound ground beef

Kosher salt

¼ teaspoon ground black pepper

1 pound cremini **mushrooms**, sliced or coarsely chopped

1 large yellow **onion** (10 ounces), coarsely chopped (2 cups)

3 **celery** stalks (6 ounces), coarsely chopped (1½ cups)

2 medium **carrots** (5 ounces), coarsely chopped (1 cup)

4 large garlic cloves

One 6-ounce can **tomato** paste

½ teaspoon dried oregano

¼ cup red wine vinegar

3 cups beef or chicken stock

1 pound pappardelle pasta

¾ cup grated Parmesan cheese (3 ounces) + more as needed

1 Heat the oil in a large pot over medium-high heat. Add the beef, spreading it out in an even layer. Sprinkle it with 1 teaspoon salt and the pepper, then allow it to cook undisturbed (yes, don't touch it!) until it is deeply browned on the pan side—6 to 8 minutes. Stir the meat and cook until the other side is brown—another 5 to 7 minutes. If the meat is not yet brown all over, continue cooking, stirring only occasionally. Once the meat is browned, scoop it out of the pot and set it aside (no need to clean the pot).

2 While the meat cooks, prepare the veggies. Process half of the mushrooms in a food processor, pulsing until finely chopped, then add the remaining mushrooms and pulse again until all the mushrooms are finely chopped. Transfer the mushrooms to the pot used to cook the beef.

3 Pulse the onion, celery, carrots, and garlic in the food processor until they are finely chopped, then add them to the pot with the mushrooms. Add another 1 teaspoon salt to the pot and continue cooking over medium-high heat until the veggies are browned and reduced in size by two-thirds—about 20 minutes. As with the beef, don't stir the veggies too frequently; by the end of the 20 minutes, you should have brown bits of food stuck to the bottom of the pot (this is a good thing!).

4 Add the tomato paste and oregano to the pot and cook for 2 minutes. Add the red wine vinegar and cook, scraping the bottom of the pot, until it is almost completely

CONTINUED . . .

. . . CONTINUED

absorbed—about 2 minutes. Then return the meat to the pot.

5 Stir in the stock and scrape the bottom of the pot to get any brown bits off and incorporate them into the sauce. Turn the heat down to medium and cook, partially covered (to avoid splatters), until the sauce is thickened and the flavors have had time to mingle—about 30 minutes. If it's not time for dinner yet, feel free to continue to cook on the stovetop until you're ready to serve; just keep adding water as needed. Thirty minutes is enough time to make a great Bolognese, but it only gets better the longer it cooks.

6 While the sauce cooks, place a large pot of salted water over high heat for cooking the pasta. When the water boils, add the pasta and cook according to the package directions until al dente. When the pasta is done, drain, reserving 2 cups of the cooking water.

7 Add the drained pasta, 1 cup of the reserved pasta water, and the Parmesan to the pot with the sauce. Give it all a good stir and let it cook for a minute to allow the pasta and sauce to marry, adding more of the reserved cooking water if the sauce is too thick. Now is the time to taste and perfect—add salt if necessary, a sprinkle more of Parm if desired, and a drizzle more of olive oil if needed.

8 Serve up the Bolognese and sprinkle each dish with a little more Parm and another drizzle of olive oil.

SWAP IT

Got some red wine on hand? Add 1 cup red wine instead of the red wine vinegar for an even richer flavor. And since you've now got an open bottle, pour yourself a glass and taste how beautifully it pairs with this cozy sauce.

chicken cauliflower alfredo

When I came up with the genius idea to make an Alfredo sauce using cauliflower, I Googled to see whether anyone else had ever tried it. My huge list of results quickly reminded me that in a world of almost 8 billion people, it's hard to have an original idea. And while it had been done before, it didn't seem like it had been done in a way that realistically could take the place of a creamy, rich Alfredo. The Alfredo sauces I found online were all basically pureed cauliflower with salt . . . um, yum?

So I'm keeping all the cauliflower in there—a whole head, actually—but I'm also adding some of that cheese and cream that make Alfredo, well, Alfredo. When all is said and done, you'll be hearing a chorus of "yums" around your dinner table.

SERVES 4

---

1 medium head **cauliflower** (1½ pounds), chopped (8 cups)

3 cups chicken stock

6 garlic cloves, smashed

4 ounces cream cheese

1 cup grated Parmesan cheese (4 ounces)

½ cup heavy cream

Kosher salt

Ground black pepper

1 pound fettuccine or linguine

1 tablespoon olive oil

2 boneless, skinless chicken breasts (12 ounces)

2 tablespoons + 2 tablespoons coarsely chopped fresh parsley, divided

1 Place a large pot of salted water over high heat for cooking the pasta. In a second large pot, bring the cauliflower, chicken stock, and garlic to a simmer, then lower the heat to medium and cook uncovered until the cauliflower is very soft—about 12 minutes.

2 Transfer the mixture to a blender and let the blender run for 1 to 2 minutes (as long as you can without stressing your machine, as some can run longer than others), until the mixture is very smooth. Transfer it back to the pot and continue cooking over medium heat to thicken the puree by about one-third—about 15 minutes. Add the cream cheese, Parmesan cheese, heavy cream, 1½ teaspoons salt, and ½ teaspoon pepper, and stir until the cheese is melted and all ingredients are combined.

3 When the water boils, add the pasta and cook according to the package directions; drain when done, reserving 1 cup of the pasta cooking water. If the drained pasta needs to sit while you finish the sauce, toss it with a drizzle of olive oil to prevent it from sticking together.

4 Meanwhile, cook the chicken. Heat the oil in a small skillet over medium heat. Sprinkle ½ teaspoon salt and ¼ teaspoon pepper evenly all over the chicken. Place the chicken in the skillet and cook until it is golden brown on both

CONTINUED . . .

step 2

...CONTINUED

sides and cooked through—about 6 minutes per side. Transfer the chicken to a cutting board to rest for 3 to 4 minutes, then slice it into ½-inch-thick pieces.

5 Fold the cauliflower sauce and 2 tablespoons of the parsley into the drained pasta. Taste it and add more salt if necessary (with so much cauliflower in the dish, you may need quite a bit more salt than you would add to your average Alfredo sauce). Add a splash of your reserved pasta cooking water to thin the sauce if necessary; you may also need to add a splash if you are not ready to serve immediately, as the sauce will thicken as it sits.

6 To serve, divide the pasta and sauce among four bowls and top with the chicken, remaining 2 tablespoons parsley, and some extra pepper.

HACK IT

Chop 1 small head of cauliflower into florets (6 cups), then simmer covered in water or stock for about 12 minutes. Drain the cauliflower and blend, along with one 15-ounce jar of store-bought Alfredo sauce and ½ teaspoon salt, in a blender until smooth. Taste and add more salt if needed. If you find the cauliflower flavor too strong, sprinkling in some Parm really helps hide it completely. Makes 3 cups sauce.

I head of
cauliflower

spaghetti squash alfredo

Because I'm a pasta fanatic, it takes a lot to sell me on a veggie noodle. I often find myself missing my traditional pasta loves and end up late-night texting my faves, penne, linguine, and of course, bucatini. It all ends up being very dramatic, so nine times out of ten, I decide to avoid all that and just eat the real thing.

My longwinded point is that if I'm giving you a veggie noodle, it's a *great* one. Spaghetti squash noodles are slightly sweet and have a bit of a bite to them. They are fine with marinara sauce, but when covered in a homemade Alfredo sauce, they really sing. Get ready for some comfort food personified while being *loaded* with veggies.

— MAKES 4 CUPS; SERVES 2 TO 4 —

1 medium-large **spaghetti squash** (2½ pounds)

1 tablespoon olive oil

Kosher salt

Ground black pepper

4 tablespoons unsalted butter

4 garlic cloves, minced

1 cup heavy cream

1 cup grated Parmesan cheese (4 ounces)

1 teaspoon finely chopped fresh parsley

1 Preheat the oven to 425°F. Now, let's cut some squash! Use a sharp chef's knife; a serrated knife works well too, as the ridges grab on to the squash. Cut off the ends of the squash, then cut the squash in half lengthwise. Use a soupspoon to scoop out the seeds, just like you would with a pumpkin, and discard them. Arrange the squash cut-side-up on a rimmed baking sheet. Drizzle the oil evenly over the squash and sprinkle it with 1 teaspoon salt and ¼ teaspoon pepper. Bake the squash until the flesh is tender and can be easily separated with the tines of a fork—35 to 40 minutes; then set it aside to cool slightly.

2 While the squash cools, prepare the sauce. Melt the butter in a large saucepan over medium-low heat, then add the garlic and sauté until it is soft and fragrant—about 5 minutes. Stir in the cream, then add the Parmesan and continue stirring until the cheese is fully melted and incorporated—about 3 minutes.

3 When the squash is cool enough to handle, use a dinner fork to gently separate the flesh into spaghetti-like strands (this should give you about 6 cups of "noodles"). Transfer the squash strands to the pan with the sauce and toss to combine. Add another ¼ teaspoon pepper and taste to see if it needs more salt; I often add another ½ to 1 teaspoon here.

4 To serve, divide the spaghetti squash Alfredo evenly among serving plates, then garnish with the parsley and additional pepper if desired.

HACK IT

Cook up your spaghetti squash as described in Step 1. Scoop out the spaghetti-like strands with a fork and transfer them to a medium pot with an additional ½ teaspoon kosher salt, ¼ teaspoon pepper, and a 15-ounce jar of store-bought Alfredo sauce. Warm everything through, adding more salt, pepper, and a sprinkle of Parm if desired.

EVEN MORE VEGGIES!

I like to top my SS Alfredo with charred broccoli, roasted hot and sweet peppers, or some fresh diced tomatoes.

cauliflower + potato gnocchi

Gnocchi is a fun one; it's a homemade pasta that doesn't involve special flours or long rest time. It's traditionally made with potatoes, but I'm bringing cauliflower into the picture too. And unlike the original recipe, where your only option is rolling and cutting and rolling and cutting until your kids are officially HANGRY, my version offers a better way. For this gnocchi, you can roll the dough out into a big rectangle, cut it into squares with a pizza wheel, and call it a day. Instead of spending time rolling and cutting, you can take the time to crisp these up so they are toasty on the outside and pillowy soft on the inside (my favorite way to have them). I think you're making gnocchi tonight, right?

MAKES ¼ POUND; SERVES 4

1 large russet potato
(12 ounces)

3 cups **cauliflower rice**, fresh or frozen (10 ounces)

2 large eggs

1 cup all-purpose flour + more as needed

¼ cup grated Parmesan cheese (1 ounce)

1½ teaspoons kosher salt

1 tablespoon olive oil + more as needed

1 Prick the skin of the potato all over with a fork. Microwave the potato on high for 5 minutes, turn over, and then microwave for another 3 minutes. If needed, keep microwaving in 1-minute bursts until done. Or if you prefer, bake at 425°F for 50 to 60 minutes.

2 Fill a large pot with salted water, and bring it to a boil over high heat for cooking the gnocchi.

3 While the potato cooks, fill a medium pot with water and bring it to a boil, then add the cauliflower rice and cook until very tender—about 10 minutes. Drain with a fine-mesh sieve, run some cool water over the cauliflower to cool it down for the next step, and let that water drain. Transfer the cauliflower rice to a clean kitchen towel. Wrap it in the towel, then twist and squeeze the towel to remove as much liquid as you can from the cauliflower.

4 When the potato is cool enough to handle, peel the skin off with a spoon and place the flesh in a medium bowl. Mash with a potato masher or fork, or run the potato through a ricer for an extra-fluffy end result.

5 Add the cauliflower and eggs to the mashed potato and mix to combine. Then add the flour, Parmesan, and salt to the bowl. Use a spoon and then your hands to mix the ingredients to form them into a dough, adding 2 more tablespoons of flour at a time, if needed, until the dough is

CONTINUED . . .

smooth and no longer sticky (it's okay if it's a little wet and tacky, but it shouldn't be sticky). Try to avoid overworking the dough, as the more you work it, the tougher the gnocchi will be.

6 Roll the dough out into a rectangle on a lightly floured surface until it is about ¾ inch thick. Using a pizza wheel, slice the dough vertically into ¾-inch-wide strips, then horizontally into ¾-inch squares. (If you prefer, you can also use the traditional method of rolling the gnocchi dough into logs, then cutting them into bite-sized pieces.)

7 Prepare a baking sheet by drizzling it with the oil. Place half of the gnocchi into the now-boiling water. Cook the gnocchi until they float to the surface of the water—about 3 minutes. Scoop them out with a slotted spoon or strainer and place them on the prepared baking sheet. Repeat this process with the remaining gnocchi.

8 To serve, toss the gnocchi with your favorite sauce. Alternatively, you can crisp up the gnocchi—my favorite way to eat them. Heat 1 tablespoon oil in a large skillet over medium-high heat, then cook the gnocchi, working in batches if necessary and adding more oil if needed, until they are brown and crispy on all sides—about 5 minutes.

SERVING SUGGESTION

To serve the crispy gnocchi, I like to add an extra drizzle of olive oil, a sprinkle of Parm, and some wilted spinach, but you can add any veggies you like.

eggplant marinara sauce

If you've ever inhaled an entire dish of eggplant Parm, you already know that eggplant and tomatoes are great together. Here, roasting and pureeing eggplant brings out a rich, slightly smoky flavor and silky texture. Add that to tomato sauce for a creamy result that balances out the acid while still allowing for that classic tomato flavor. I don't know about your house, but eggplant is not a typical side dish around here, so I love that we can all enjoy it in a whole new way.

--- MAKES 4 CUPS ---

1 medium **eggplant** (1 pound)

1 tablespoon + ¼ cup olive oil, divided

1 small yellow **onion** (5 ounces), finely chopped (1 cup)

5 garlic cloves, minced

Kosher salt

Two 28-ounce cans crushed **tomatoes**

¼ teaspoon ground black pepper

1–2 teaspoons granulated sugar (optional)

3 tablespoons finely chopped fresh basil leaves

1 Preheat the oven to 425°F. Cut the eggplant in half lengthwise and place the halves cut-side-up on a rimmed baking sheet. Drizzle them with 1 tablespoon of the oil and bake until very soft—about 30 minutes. Remove the eggplant from the oven and set aside to cool.

2 While the eggplant roasts, heat the remaining ¼ cup oil in a large pot over medium heat. Add the onion, garlic, and ½ teaspoon salt and cook until the veggies are fragrant and tender—about 10 minutes.

3 Add the tomatoes, 1 teaspoon salt, and the pepper. Simmer uncovered until the mixture thickens a bit and the flavors come together—another 15 minutes.

4 When the eggplant is cool enough to handle, use a spoon to scrape its flesh into a food processor or blender, then process until it is very smooth (giving you about 1 cup puree). If you have any trouble getting the eggplant to blend in the blender, add some of the tomatoes or a splash of water.

5 Stir the eggplant puree into the tomato sauce until incorporated, then taste the sauce and add more salt if needed; this will depend on how salty your brand of canned tomatoes is. Some chefs also like to add a bit of sugar, so if you think your sauce is too acidic, add 1 to 2 teaspoons. Stir the basil into the sauce, then serve as desired.

CONTINUED . . .

step 2

step 4

step 5

... **CONTINUED**

HACK IT

Cook the eggplant as described in Step 1, then puree it in a food processor or blender; this should give you 1 cup eggplant puree. Combine the eggplant puree, ½ teaspoon salt, and a 24-ounce jar of your favorite marinara sauce in a medium pot; heat and serve with pasta. Note, if using a blender, you may need to add some of the jarred sauce along with the eggplant to give your blender enough liquid to puree it all up.

FREEZE IT

Freeze in 1-cup portions for up to 5 months. I like a lot of sauce on my pasta and generally use 1 cup of sauce for every ¼ pound of pasta.

basil spinach pesto

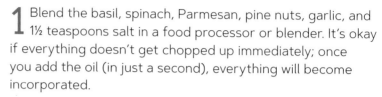

For whatever reason, many kids like pesto. Even in its green glory, most kids are fine with that herbal flavor. In fact, all three of my kids love it. It's a miracle! So if pesto is a staple in your home, I want to give you a recipe that makes a simple pesto even better, and even better for you. Time to throw some spinach in the mix and make your pasta even more green!

— MAKES 1¾ CUPS —

3 cups fresh basil leaves
(3 ounces)

3 cups **baby spinach**
(3 ounces)

1 cup grated Parmesan
cheese (4 ounces)

¼ cup pine nuts (1½ ounces)

1 garlic clove, peeled

Kosher salt

½ cup olive oil + more as
needed

1 Blend the basil, spinach, Parmesan, pine nuts, garlic, and 1½ teaspoons salt in a food processor or blender. It's okay if everything doesn't get chopped up immediately; once you add the oil (in just a second), everything will become incorporated.

2 With the machine still running, slowly add the oil. The amount of oil I call for is on the low side, so if you prefer to add a touch more, go for it!

3 Taste the pesto, then add more salt if necessary. (If your plan is to toss your pesto with pasta, I prefer to wait and test my salt after tossing the pesto and pasta together. Sometimes I find it hard to tell if the salt is right until the warm pasta allows the garlic to cook slightly, the Parm to melt, and the basil and spinach to wilt a little.)

TO SERVE WITH PASTA

Toss the pesto with hot pasta, adding a splash of the pasta cooking water to marry everything together. Taste and add more salt if necessary. Sometimes for my husband and me, I'll also toss the pasta with a little extra olive oil from my high-quality stash. This amount of pesto could be used for 1 to 2 pounds of pasta, depending on how saucy you like your pasta.

OTHER SERVING OPTIONS

There are so many ways to enjoy this pesto. You can use it as an awesome spread for sandwiches; you can mix it with mayo for a spread for my Ultimate Veggie Burgers (page 145); you can use it instead of tomato sauce on my Zucchini Crust Pizza (page 155); or you can even just toss a spoonful with your scrambled eggs. The world is your oyster!

HACK IT

Simply put one container of store-bought pesto (usually between 6 and 8 ounces) in a food processor with 3 to 4 cups (3 to 4 ounces) baby spinach. Add a pinch of salt and blend until mostly smooth. I usually start with 3 cups spinach, taste, then add more if I think I can get away with it. I also taste and add more salt as needed. I often find that this hack vastly improves the store-bought stuff in both taste and color. It's a great one!

STORE IT + FREEZE IT

Store pesto in the fridge for up to a week or freeze your pesto in the compartments of an ice cube tray; for pasta, pop out one cube for kid portions and two to three for an adult portion.

SWAP IT

*Replace the pine nuts with walnuts, pecans, or almonds.
It's even okay to just leave them out entirely.*

½ basil,
½ spinach

penne alla vodka

When I've got that comfort-food itch, this pasta does the scratching. Penne alla vodka used to be my go-to restaurant order. But that all changed when I started making this dish at home—in just 15 minutes! And while playing with the recipe in my kitchen, I found the key ingredient to balancing the tang of the tomatoes and making an ultra-creamy sauce—zucchini.

"Okay, Nikki, it's fast and zucchini is vital, but why the vodka?" Although you won't taste the alcohol, it plays an important role in revealing flavors and aromas that would otherwise remain undercover. It also creates an emulsifying bridge among the zucchini, cream, and tomatoes, encouraging them to work together to make this sauce extra smooth and velvety. However, if you prefer to keep the vodka in your glass and out of your pasta, just omit it—it will still be an easy tomato-forward sauce your kids are sure to ask for again and again.

— SERVES 6 —

3 tablespoons unsalted butter

1 medium **zucchini** (9 ounces), chopped (2 cups)

1 medium yellow **onion** (8 ounces), chopped (1½ cups)

5 garlic cloves, sliced

Kosher salt

¾ cup heavy cream

1 pound penne

One 8-ounce can **tomato** sauce

One 6-ounce can **tomato** paste

¼ cup vodka

¼ cup grated Parmesan cheese (1 ounce) + more for a garnish

¼ teaspoon red pepper flakes + more as needed (optional)

2 tablespoons finely chopped fresh basil leaves + more for a garnish

1 Place a large pot of salted water over high heat for cooking the penne. Melt the butter in another large pot over medium heat, then add the zucchini, onion, garlic, and 1 teaspoon salt. Cook until the veggies are very tender—7 to 10 minutes. Transfer this mixture to a blender along with the cream and blend until it is very smooth, then set aside.

2 When the water boils, add the penne and cook according to the package directions. When done, drain, reserving 1½ cups of the cooking water. If your pasta needs to sit, stir a splash of olive oil into the drained pasta so that it doesn't stick together as it sits, then set aside.

3 In the now-empty pot you used to cook the veggies, cook the tomato sauce, tomato paste, and vodka over medium heat, stirring occasionally, until the liquid has evaporated and the mixture is thicker and darker in color—5 to 7 minutes. Add the blended zucchini-cream mixture to the pot along with the Parmesan, another ½ teaspoon salt, and red pepper flakes (if desired) and stir well to combine. Taste the sauce and add more salt if needed, and more red pepper flakes if you want it spicier.

4 Add the pasta to the sauce along with ½ cup of the reserved pasta water, stir to combine, and cook for 1 minute more (add more pasta water to thin out the sauce if it's too thick). Add the basil and stir.

CONTINUED . . .

step 1

step 3

. . . CONTINUED

5 Serve the pasta garnished with more Parmesan, basil, and red pepper flakes (if desired).

NOTE

Although many will tell you that all the alcohol cooks out of a dish like this, that's not exactly true—there is a small amount left behind. So although I do love the role the vodka plays here, if you'd rather not serve this dish as is to your family, you can always simply skip the vodka.

pumpkin pasta dough

Two important things to note: (1) It doesn't taste like pumpkin; it just tastes like awesome homemade pasta with an addictive firm but tender bite. (2) It's easy, I promise. Many people are intimidated when they think about making homemade pasta, but I've taken the guesswork out of it. You don't even need a pasta machine! It is perfect for when you've got an itch to make something from scratch, and works well as a fun recipe to make with kids (Ivy especially loves helping with anything involving a dough). There is a little work, but the payoff is really big.

──────── MAKES 2½ POUNDS; SERVES 8 ────────

One 15-ounce can pure **pumpkin** puree (1¾ cups)

1 large egg

2 teaspoons kosher salt

4½ cups all-purpose flour + more as needed

SWAP IT

Replace the pumpkin with butternut squash puree; look for a 15-ounce can next to the other canned veggies in your grocery store. Or use 1¾ cups homemade puree.

1 Prepare a baking sheet by sprinkling it lightly with flour.

BY HAND: Whisk the pumpkin puree, egg, and salt together in a large bowl. Add the flour and stir the ingredients together with a wooden spoon until a rough dough comes together.

MIXER: Use a dough hook attachment to blend the pumpkin and egg together first; then add the flour and salt and mix until everything comes together into a mostly smooth ball; you may need to scrape the bottom of the bowl halfway through. This should take about 3 minutes on medium speed (the mixer is my favorite method—it saves you an arm workout in the next step).

2 Knead the dough on a lightly floured work surface until it is smooth and forms a ball, adding more flour if the dough is sticky; this will take about 5 minutes if you stirred the dough by hand, 1 minute if you made it in the mixer. It's okay if the dough ball is not perfectly smooth.

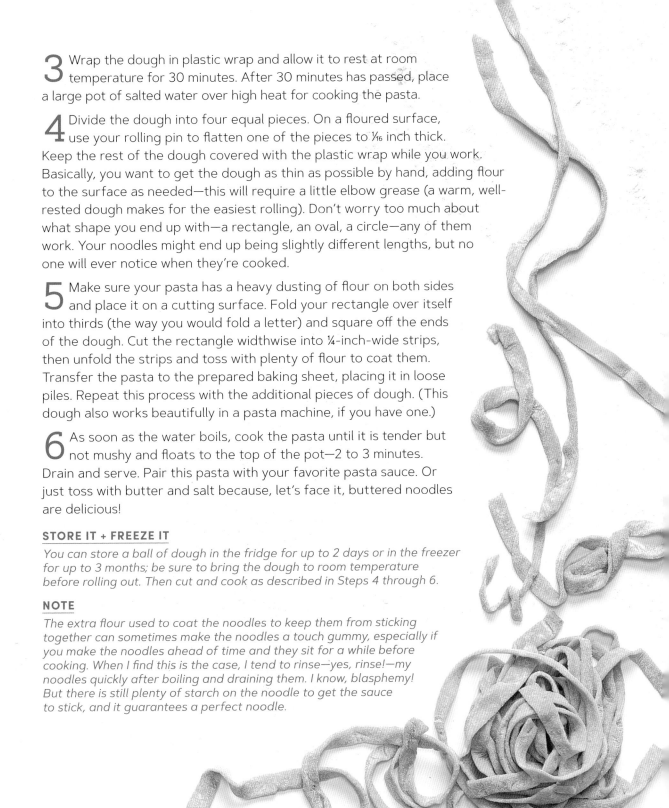

3 Wrap the dough in plastic wrap and allow it to rest at room temperature for 30 minutes. After 30 minutes has passed, place a large pot of salted water over high heat for cooking the pasta.

4 Divide the dough into four equal pieces. On a floured surface, use your rolling pin to flatten one of the pieces to ⅟₁₆ inch thick. Keep the rest of the dough covered with the plastic wrap while you work. Basically, you want to get the dough as thin as possible by hand, adding flour to the surface as needed—this will require a little elbow grease (a warm, well-rested dough makes for the easiest rolling). Don't worry too much about what shape you end up with—a rectangle, an oval, a circle—any of them work. Your noodles might end up being slightly different lengths, but no one will ever notice when they're cooked.

5 Make sure your pasta has a heavy dusting of flour on both sides and place it on a cutting surface. Fold your rectangle over itself into thirds (the way you would fold a letter) and square off the ends of the dough. Cut the rectangle widthwise into ¼-inch-wide strips, then unfold the strips and toss with plenty of flour to coat them. Transfer the pasta to the prepared baking sheet, placing it in loose piles. Repeat this process with the additional pieces of dough. (This dough also works beautifully in a pasta machine, if you have one.)

6 As soon as the water boils, cook the pasta until it is tender but not mushy and floats to the top of the pot—2 to 3 minutes. Drain and serve. Pair this pasta with your favorite pasta sauce. Or just toss with butter and salt because, let's face it, buttered noodles are delicious!

STORE IT + FREEZE IT
You can store a ball of dough in the fridge for up to 2 days or in the freezer for up to 3 months; be sure to bring the dough to room temperature before rolling out. Then cut and cook as described in Steps 4 through 6.

NOTE
The extra flour used to coat the noodles to keep them from sticking together can sometimes make the noodles a touch gummy, especially if you make the noodles ahead of time and they sit for a while before cooking. When I find this is the case, I tend to rinse—yes, rinse!—my noodles quickly after boiling and draining them. I know, blasphemy! But there is still plenty of starch on the noodle to get the sauce to stick, and it guarantees a perfect noodle.

Spinach Pasta Dough
(page 126)

Pumpkin Pasta Dough
(page 122)

spinach pasta dough

Nothing in life makes me happier than a big bowl of pasta. And when I can get my side of veggies and pasta in one bite, well, you know I'm sneaking back to the stove for seconds and thirds. For this recipe, I'm tossing a box of spinach into the food processor to create a velvety puree, then adding it to a two-ingredient dough. The noodles are tender while still having that addictive al dente bite. Toss with marinara sauce or—for a super green and spinach-filled dinner—my Basil Spinach Pesto (page 116). Call it Dinosaur Pasta and they'll come running!

—————————————— MAKES 1½ POUNDS; SERVES 6 ——————————————

One 10-ounce package
   frozen chopped **spinach**
2 large eggs
2 teaspoons kosher salt
4 cups all-purpose flour

1 Prepare a baking sheet by sprinkling it lightly with flour. Thaw the spinach by microwaving it for 1 to 3 minutes, but do not squeeze out any of the excess liquid (the liquid helps the dough come together and is full of nutrients). Process the spinach in a food processor along with the eggs and salt, blending the mixture until the spinach is very smooth and scraping down the bowl as needed.

2 <u>FOOD PROCESSOR</u>: Add the flour to the food processor and blend until the mixture comes together to form a dough that is barely sticky. If the mixture is crumbly, add 2 tablespoons water at a time, blending again until the dough comes together. Knead the dough on a lightly floured work surface until it is smooth and forms a ball, adding more flour if the dough is sticky; this will take about 2 minutes. It's okay if the dough ball is not perfectly smooth.

<u>MIXER:</u> Use a dough hook attachment to combine the spinach mixture and flour until they come together into a mostly smooth ball; you may need to scrape the bottom of the bowl halfway through. This should take about 3 minutes on medium speed.

3 Wrap the dough in plastic wrap and allow it to rest at room temperature for 30 minutes. After 30 minutes has passed, place a large pot of salted water over high heat for cooking the pasta.

4 Divide the dough into four equal pieces. On a floured surface, use your rolling pin to flatten one of the pieces to ¹⁄₁₆ inch thick. Keep the rest of the dough covered with the plastic wrap while you work. Basically, you want to get the dough as thin as possible by hand, adding flour to the surface as needed—this will require a little elbow grease. Don't worry too much about what shape you end up with—a rectangle, an oval, a circle—any of them work. Your noodles might end up being slightly different lengths, but no one will ever notice.

5 Make sure your pasta has a heavy dusting of flour on both sides and place it on a cutting surface. Fold your rectangle over itself into thirds (the way you would fold a letter) and square off the ends of the dough. Cut the rectangle widthwise into ¼-inch-wide strips, then unfold the strips and toss with more flour to coat them. Transfer the pasta to the prepared baking sheet, placing it in loose piles. Repeat this process with the additional pieces of dough. (This dough also works beautifully in a pasta machine, if you have one.)

6 As soon as the water boils, cook the pasta until it is tender but not mushy and floats to the top of the pot—2 to 3 minutes. Drain and serve with your favorite sauce.

STORE IT + FREEZE IT

You can store a ball of dough in the fridge for up to 2 days or in the freezer for up to 3 months; be sure to bring the dough to room temperature before rolling out. Then cut and cook as described in Steps 4 through 6.

NOTE

If you find your noodles are a bit gummy from the excess flour, consider rinsing them after cooking and draining. This helps make the texture perfect, and the noodles will still marry wonderfully with any sauce you throw at them.

eggplant parm meatballs

We call Daisy the Meatball Monster—she *loves* meatballs. And she loves these ones above all others. Here, the pureed eggplant takes the place of the milk found in traditional meatballs, adding that same moistness and an extra layer of richness. And cooking up the eggplant is as easy as slicing it in half and tossing it in the oven to roast. Sometimes I'll throw an extra eggplant in the oven, puree it, and freeze it so I can whip these up even faster the next time. In case you couldn't tell, we make meatballs a lot around here.

———————— MAKES TWENTY 1½-INCH MEATBALLS ————————

1 medium **eggplant** (1 pound)

1 tablespoon + 1 tablespoon olive oil, divided

1 large egg

1 cup Italian breadcrumbs

½ cup grated Parmesan cheese (2 ounces)

1 teaspoon kosher salt

½ teaspoon onion powder

½ teaspoon garlic powder

¼ teaspoon ground black pepper

1 pound ground beef

TOPPINGS

2½ cups marinara sauce (one 24-ounce jar)

2 cups shredded mozzarella cheese (8 ounces)

Fresh basil or parsley, finely chopped, for a garnish

Red pepper flakes, for a garnish

1 Preheat the oven to 425°F. Cut the eggplant in half lengthwise and place the halves cut-side-up on a baking sheet. Drizzle the halves with 1 tablespoon of the oil and bake until they are very soft—about 30 minutes.

2 When the eggplant is cool enough to handle, use a spoon to scrape its flesh into a food processor or blender (if you are using a blender, add the egg here as well to give you enough liquid to blend with); discard the skin. Process until completely pureed; this should give you about 1 cup eggplant puree (if you don't have 1 cup, add some marinara sauce to make up the difference). If you're in a pinch and don't have a food processor or blender, a potato masher does a decent job.

3 Transfer the puree to a large bowl, then add the breadcrumbs, Parmesan, egg (unless you already added it to the blender), salt, onion powder, garlic powder, and pepper and mix until mostly combined. Add the beef to the bowl and combine the ingredients with your hands, avoiding overmixing. Form the mixture into 1½-inch balls.

4 Heat the remaining 1 tablespoon oil in a large skillet over medium heat. Place the meatballs in the skillet and brown them on all sides, cooking until the centers are no longer pink—about 15 minutes. (Alternatively, you can bake the meatballs on a cooking oil–sprayed baking sheet at 400°F for about 15 minutes. Cook for one additional minute under the broiler for extra color.)

5 Preheat the broiler to high. Place the cooked meatballs in a serving dish that can go in the oven and cover them with the marinara sauce and mozzarella, then broil until the cheese is melted. Top with basil or parsley and red pepper flakes, then serve and enjoy!

HACK IT

Make these super speedy by skipping the eggplant and adding 1 cup of your favorite marinara sauce instead.

FREEZE IT

Freeze just the cooked meatballs (not the whole dish covered in sauce and cheese), once they have cooled completely. To thaw, bake them at 350°F for 10 to 15 minutes. Alternatively, you can microwave the meatballs for 1 to 3 minutes, depending on how many are on your plate. To serve with sauce and cheese, once the meatballs are warm, continue with Step 5.

sweet potato pie crust
+ beans inside

chicken pot pie
with sweet potato crust

Chicken pot pie is already chock full of veggies, but now we're really upping the ante. With this recipe, you'll be adding beans to the sauce for the perfect amount of creaminess, plus topping it all with a perfectly flaky, tender, and crispy sweet potato crust. Yum! It's an old-school dish that you can feel really good about adding to your rotation.

--- SERVES 8 ---

SWEET POTATO CRUST

1 small **sweet potato** (5 ounces)

3 cups all-purpose flour

2 teaspoons kosher salt

1½ teaspoons baking powder

¾ cup cold unsalted butter (1½ sticks), cut into ½-inch cubes

CHICKEN POT PIE

4 tablespoons unsalted butter

1 large yellow **onion** (10 ounces), finely chopped (2 cups)

2 medium **carrots** (5 ounces), finely chopped (1 cup)

2 large **celery** stalks (4½ ounces), finely chopped (1¼ cups)

Kosher salt

One 15-ounce can **cannellini beans**, drained + rinsed

1 cup whole milk

½ cup all-purpose flour

1 tablespoon finely chopped fresh thyme leaves

2 cups chicken stock

1 teaspoon garlic powder

4 cups shredded rotisserie chicken (1 pound)

2 cups frozen **peas** (10 ounces)

Ground black pepper

TOPPING

1 large egg

TO MAKE THE CRUST:

1 Poke several holes in the sweet potato with a fork. Cook the sweet potato in the microwave on high until very soft—5 to 7 minutes.

2 Remove the sweet potato from the microwave and allow it to cool. Once it is cool enough to handle, cut it in half, scoop its flesh into the bowl of a food processor, and add 2 tablespoons water. Process until the sweet potato becomes a smooth puree; when finished, you should have about ½ cup puree. Transfer the sweet potato puree to a bowl (no need to clean out the food processor), then chill it in the freezer while you prep the other ingredients; if it's too hot, it will melt the butter in your crust, which will prevent the crust from turning out nice and flaky.

3 Pulse the flour, salt, and baking powder in the food processor until fully combined. Then add the butter and pulse until the mixture resembles coarse breadcrumbs. Remove the chilled sweet potato puree from the freezer, transfer it back into the food

CONTINUED . . .

processor, and pulse until all the ingredients are combined and the mixture forms a rough dough.

4 Knead the dough on a lightly floured work surface a couple of times until it comes together. Wrap the dough in plastic wrap and chill it in your refrigerator until it is firm but still easy to roll out—about 30 minutes. While it chills, prepare and cook your filling.

TO MAKE THE CHICKEN POT PIE:

1 Preheat the oven to 425°F. Melt the butter in a large pot over medium heat. Add the onion, carrots, celery, and ½ teaspoon salt and cook until the veggies just begin to soften—7 to 10 minutes. While the veggies cook, blend the cannellini beans and milk in a blender or food processor until very smooth.

2 Add the flour and thyme to the pot with the veggies and cook, whisking until the flour is completely incorporated and the thyme is fragrant—about 2 minutes (I know sometimes you can sub in a different tool for the job, but this time—and for the next step—you really do need a whisk).

3 Transfer the bean and milk puree to the pot with the veggies, along with the chicken stock and garlic powder. Whisk very well to fully incorporate the flour into the milk and stock. Bring the mixture to a boil, reduce it to a simmer, and cook, stirring frequently, until thickened—about 5 minutes. Turn off the heat and stir in the chicken, peas, another 1 teaspoon salt, and some pepper. Now taste! The filling is fully done, so this is your chance to adjust the seasoning as you like; add more thyme, salt, or pepper according to your preference. Pour the mixture into a 13 × 9-inch baking dish (or divide it evenly between two pie pans) and allow it to cool slightly while you roll out your Sweet Potato Crust.

4 Remove the Sweet Potato Crust from the refrigerator and place it on a lightly floured surface. Shape it with your hands into a rough rectangle, then roll it into a large rectangle that is at least 14 × 10 inches (so that it is larger than the baking dish) and ⅛ inch thick. Lay the Sweet Potato Crust on top of the baking dish, pressing the dough lightly onto the filling. Trim any excess dough, leaving an overhang of 1 inch of dough on all sides. Pinch or crimp the edge of the dough as desired.

5 Whisk the egg and 1 tablespoon water in a small bowl until combined. Brush the dough with the egg wash, then cut three 1-inch slits in the center of the crust to allow the steam to release.

6 Place the baking dish on a baking sheet (in case it bubbles over) and bake the pot pie in the oven, until the crust is golden brown and the filling is bubbling around the edges—about 45 minutes. Allow the pot pie to stand for 15 minutes before serving.

FREEZE IT

You can freeze the complete but unbaked pot pie (minus the egg wash in Step 5) in the 13 × 9-inch baking dish. Cover it with foil and freeze for up to 5 months. To thaw, bake the frozen dish, still covered with the foil, at 425°F for 50 minutes. Once the pot pie is thawed, remove the foil, brush the crust with the egg wash as described in Step 5, and continue cooking at 425°F until the filling is bubbling and hot and the crust is brown—30 to 40 minutes more. Alternatively, I like to split the pot pie and crust into two disposable pie dishes, cover in foil and freeze. The smaller size is a little better for our family and takes up less room in the freezer. For this method, thaw by cooking covered with the foil for 30 minutes at 425°F, then remove the foil, brush the crust with the egg wash as described in Step 5, and continue to cook for 30 to 40 minutes more.

SWAP IT

Replace the cannellini beans with any light-colored bean; even chickpeas work here.

cauliflower chive risotto

When you take your first bite of this ultra-dreamy rice dish, you'll be convinced that it is laden with cream and butter. In actuality, that richness comes from extra-starchy Arborio rice, a staple for making risotto (and don't fret, it's easily found at your market). The more you stir this special rice, the more the starch releases, making it creamier and creamier on the outside while still staying tender yet firm on the inside—it's what comfort-food dreams are made of. Add some cauliflower rice, which blends in perfectly because of its similar firm-tender bite, and you'll officially be on cloud nine.

MAKES 4 CUPS; SERVES 4

1 quart chicken or vegetable stock

2 tablespoons olive oil

1 medium yellow onion (8 ounces), finely chopped (1½ cups)

3 garlic cloves, minced

Kosher salt

1 cup Arborio rice

2 cups **cauliflower rice**, fresh or frozen (6 ounces; see notes)

Ground black pepper

1¼ cups grated Parmesan cheese (5 ounces)

¼ cup finely chopped fresh chives + more for a garnish

¼ teaspoon red pepper flakes (optional)

1 Warm the stock in a small saucepan over low heat. While it warms, heat the oil in a large skillet over medium heat. Add the onion, garlic, and ½ teaspoon salt to the oil in the skillet and cook until the onion is soft and translucent—about 5 minutes. Add the Arborio rice to the onion in the skillet and continue cooking until the rice is just toasted—about 5 minutes more.

2 Gradually add the warmed stock to the vegetable and rice mixture, ½ cup at a time, stirring often and waiting until it is fully absorbed before adding more. Continue until the rice is just tender, but still shy of al dente—15 to 20 minutes. If at any point you run out of stock, you can use water.

3 Stir in the cauliflower rice, ½ cup more stock (or water, if needed), another ¼ teaspoon salt, and ¼ teaspoon pepper. Cook, stirring often, until the cauliflower is tender and the rice is al dente—10 to 15 minutes.

4 Add the Parmesan, chives, and red pepper flakes (if desired). Continue to cook, stirring, until the cheese is melted and the ingredients are well combined. Taste and add more salt if necessary. If your risotto thickens too much as you prepare to serve it, add a splash more stock or water. Garnish with chives and a sprinkle of black pepper, and enjoy!

NOTES

* Got some wine on hand? After the rice is toasted at the end of Step 1, add ½ cup white wine (a traditional ingredient in risotto) and cook until it is absorbed by the rice. Then continue on with Steps 2 and 3, adding the stock, cauliflower rice, and so on. Get ready for a great flavor boost!

* To make homemade cauliflower rice, process half of a small head of cauliflower (9 ounces). That should give you the 2 cups you need for this recipe.

breaded with eggplant, not egg

chicken parmesan

Over the years, my love of veggies has evolved into a sort of philosophy: I believe that veggies not only are amazing on their own but also have the ability to intensify flavors, amplify traditional recipes, and take your cooking to the next level.

This chicken Parm is a great example. The veggie twist here is that I'm using eggplant instead of egg to stick the breading to the chicken. But it's not just a simple substitute for the sake of getting a veggie into the recipe; the roasted eggplant brings a subtle smoky, savory quality, adding a depth of flavor that makes all the difference. Bottom line, recipes with veggie twists aren't just *as good* as their nonveggie versions—they're better.

_____ SERVES 4 _____

1 medium **eggplant**
   (1 pound)
1 tablespoon olive oil
Kosher salt
Ground black pepper
4 small boneless, skinless
   chicken breasts
   (1½ pounds total)
1½ cups panko breadcrumbs
½ cup **wheat germ**
1½ teaspoons Italian
   seasoning
1 teaspoon garlic powder
1 teaspoon onion powder
½ cup all-purpose flour
Canola oil, for pan-frying
1 cup + 1 cup shredded
   mozzarella cheese, divided
   (8 ounces total)
1 cup marinara sauce
¼ cup grated Parmesan
   cheese (1 ounce)
2 tablespoons chopped
   fresh parsley, for a
   garnish

1 Preheat the oven to 425°F. Cut the eggplant in half lengthwise and place the halves cut-side-up on a rimmed baking sheet. Drizzle them lightly with the olive oil, then sprinkle with ½ teaspoon salt and ¼ teaspoon pepper. Bake the eggplant until it is very soft—about 30 minutes; then set it aside to cool slightly.

2 While the eggplant cooks, prepare the chicken. Place the chicken breasts, one at a time, into a 1-gallon plastic storage bag (you can also cover with a sheet of parchment paper or plastic wrap instead). Use the flat side of a meat tenderizer, a rolling pin, or a heavy frying pan to flatten the chicken out until it is a little less than ½ inch thick. Refrigerate the chicken breasts until needed.

3 When the eggplant is cool enough to handle, use a spoon to scrape its flesh into the bowl of a food processor; discard the skin. Process until the eggplant is completely pureed (this should give you about 1 cup eggplant puree), then transfer the puree to a shallow bowl. In a second shallow bowl, stir together the breadcrumbs, wheat germ, Italian seasoning, garlic powder, onion powder, and 1 teaspoon salt. Place the flour in a third shallow bowl.

4 Remove the chicken breasts from the refrigerator and season them with another 1 teaspoon salt and ¼ teaspoon pepper. Toss the chicken breasts, one at a time, in the flour, coating them completely, then shaking off any excess. Transfer the chicken to the bowl with the eggplant

CONTINUED . . .

and again coat it completely (using a pastry brush is a fast and easy way to get an even layer of coating). Next, transfer the chicken to the bowl with the breadcrumb mixture and make sure to get a good coating of the mixture by really pressing the breadcrumbs into the chicken breasts.

5 Fill a large, high-sided skillet over medium-high heat with about ¼ inch of oil, then heat the oil until it begins to shimmer. Carefully dip the tip of one of the breaded chicken breasts into the hot oil to test whether it is ready; if the oil bubbles vigorously, you're good to go; if it doesn't, wait another minute and try again. Once the oil is hot enough, cook the chicken, working in two batches, until it is golden brown and cooked through—about 4 minutes per side. Transfer the cooked chicken to a cooling rack, which will help it stay crispy as you work.

6 Arrange the chicken on a baking sheet or in a casserole dish in a single layer, then divide 1 cup of the mozzarella among the chicken breasts, sprinkling it down their centers. Spoon the marinara sauce on top of the mozzarella, then top the sauce with the remaining 1 cup mozzarella, then the Parmesan.

7 Bake until the cheese is completely melted and lightly browned in spots—10 to 15 minutes. Garnish with the parsley and serve family style.

SWAP IT

You can replace the wheat germ with ½ cup more panko breadcrumbs.

NOTE

If you end up with leftover eggplant puree, you can add it to your marinara sauce; be sure to simmer it in a small pot with the sauce for 5 minutes to cook off any raw chicken drippings.

homemade hamburger helper with squash + lentils

Many of us have fond memories of eating Hamburger Helper as kids (or of polishing off a skillet last Tuesday!). When I was young, my mom made huge batches of the stuff, and even Picky Nikki dove right in (navigating to make sure all I actually ate were the noodles, of course). But I never found myself making the dish as an adult . . . until now.

My love affair was reignited when I threw 6 cups of squash and a whole can of beans at the dish and it still tasted like comfort food exemplified. The hidden squash seamlessly melts into the cheesy, spicy sauce, and the lentils blend in so stealthily that no one will ever know half of the "meat" isn't beef. On top of that, this mouthwatering, kid-approved meal is made in one pan in less than 30 minutes.

—————— SERVES 8 ——————

6 cups peeled + cubed **butternut squash** (24 ounces), fresh or frozen

One 15-ounce can **brown lentils** or **pinto beans**, drained + rinsed

2 tablespoons olive oil

1 pound ground beef

Kosher salt

½ teaspoon ground black pepper

4–6 cups beef stock

1 pound elbow macaroni

½ cup heavy cream

2 teaspoons garlic powder

2 teaspoons paprika

1 teaspoon chili powder

2–4 cups shredded cheddar cheese (8–16 ounces)

¼ cup chopped fresh chives, + more for a garnish

1 Bring a large pot of water to a boil, add the squash, and cook until the squash is easily pierced with a fork—about 10 minutes for fresh and 2 minutes for frozen. Drain and puree the squash in a food processor or blender (this should give you about 2 cups puree) and set it aside.

2 While the squash cooks, use a fork or potato masher to mash the lentils or pinto beans until they are mostly smooth, then set aside. Return the large pot used to cook the squash to the stove, add the oil, and heat over medium-high heat. Add the beef, spreading it as best you can into an even layer. Season it with 1 teaspoon salt and the pepper, then allow the beef to cook undisturbed until it is deeply brown and crispy on the pan side—about 5 minutes.

CONTINUED . . .

3 Spread the lentils or beans on top of the browned beef, then push them down with your spoon, mashing them into the beef. Once the lentils or beans are fused into the beef, start breaking up the mixture, flipping it over to cook the other side. Continue cooking until the beef is mostly cooked through (it's okay if it's still pink in spots)—2 to 3 minutes more.

4 Add 4 cups of the beef stock, the macaroni, squash puree, cream, garlic powder, paprika, chili powder, and another 1 teaspoon salt. Stir to combine, scraping the bottom of the pot to get any brown bits up that might be stuck there. Bring the mixture to a boil and cook, stirring occasionally, until the noodles are al dente—10 to 15 minutes. If the noodles need to cook more and the liquid is gone, add more stock (or water) as needed. Also, taste and add more salt if needed.

5 Add the cheddar and stir until melted. For a more beef-forward dish, I use 2 cups cheese; for a cheesier Cheeseburger Helper–inspired dish, I use 4 cups. Once the cheese is melted and incorporated, stir in the chives and add more stock or water if the mixture is too thick. Serve hot, topped with extra chives and even a dash of hot sauce if you like it spicy.

NOTE

A splash of beef stock or plain water really helps reenergize leftovers or bring the dish back to life if it's been sitting for a while before serving. The extra liquid fully returns the dish to its saucy, creamy glory.

half meat,
half beans

6 cups of
butternut squash!

Mushroom +
Onion Burgers
(page 144)

Ultimate Veggie
Burgers (page 145)

mushroom + onion burgers

Many people aren't big mushroom fans, and that especially goes for kids. But when you properly brown mushrooms, they transform into umami bombs, making whatever you add them to intensely savory—in this case, they make the beef even beefier and keep the burgers irresistibly moist. You just might see mushrooms in a whole new light.

MAKES 4 LARGE, 6 MEDIUM, OR 8 SLIDER-STYLE BURGERS

8 ounces **baby bella mushrooms**, sliced (3 cups)

1 small yellow **onion** (5 ounces), roughly chopped (1 cup)

1 tablespoon + 1 tablespoon olive oil, divided

1 large egg

2 teaspoons kosher salt

2 teaspoons minced fresh rosemary (optional)

1 teaspoon garlic powder

1 teaspoon ground black pepper

1 pound ground beef

4 thick slices cheddar cheese (optional)

1 Preheat the oven to 425°F. Place the mushrooms and onion on a parchment-lined baking sheet. Drizzle them with 1 tablespoon of the oil, toss to coat, and spread everything out into an even layer. Roast until the mushrooms are deep brown and the onions are soft and charred in spots—25 to 30 minutes.

2 Pulse the roasted veggies in the bowl of a food processor until they are finely chopped but not completely pureed. Transfer the mixture to a medium bowl.

3 To the mushroom and onion mixture, add the egg, salt, rosemary (if desired), garlic powder, and pepper and mix until well combined. Add the beef and mix until all the ingredients just come together, avoiding overmixing. Your hands are the best tool for this job.

4 Next, form the mixture by hand into four patties about ½ inch thick (or, six or eight smaller burgers, depending on desired size). Heat the remaining 1 tablespoon oil in a large skillet over medium-high heat, then add the patties and cover the pan. Cook the burgers until the sides facing the pan are well browned—3 to 6 minutes, depending on size. Flip the burgers, then cover the pan and continue cooking for 3 to 6 minutes more. With about 1 minute remaining on the cook time, top each burger with a slice of cheddar if desired. Re-cover the pan and cook until the cheese has melted and the burgers are well browned on both sides and are cooked to medium-rare (145°F) or your desired doneness. Top as desired and enjoy!

ultimate
veggie burgers

You order a veggie burger at a restaurant. It comes to the table looking *great*. You get excited, take a bite, and . . . it squishes right out of the bun and crumbles onto the plate. You cry. End scene.

This is all too common. The problem is that vegetables contain lots of moisture and none of the binders that help a regular beef burger stay together. What's the solution? Well, we've got to draw out all that moisture to make the patty nice and firm, so we need to bake the mushrooms, beans, and rice first. This removes the excess moisture and gives you the perfect amount of space to put a little moisture back in via some essential ingredients—barbecue sauce for flavor and egg as a binder. In the end, you have *the* most delicious burger—veggie or not!—and it's so sturdy that it can even be grilled.

─── MAKES 5 BURGERS ───

One 15-ounce can **brown lentils** or **pinto beans**, drained + rinsed

8 ounces **baby bella mushrooms**, sliced (3 cups)

1½ cups cooked brown rice (see note)

½ cup walnuts, whole or pieces (optional)

¼ cup all-purpose flour

1 large egg

2 tablespoons barbecue sauce + more as needed

1 teaspoon kosher salt

1 teaspoon garlic powder

1 teaspoon finely chopped fresh rosemary (optional)

1 tablespoon olive oil

1 Preheat the oven to 400°F. Line a baking sheet with parchment paper or spray it with cooking oil spray. Spread the lentils or pinto beans over half of the baking sheet and the mushrooms over the other half. Roast until the lentils or beans are dry and crisp on the outside and the mushrooms are shrunken to half their original size—about 25 minutes.

2 Use a wooden spoon to move the mushrooms to the side, then spread the cooked rice in the open space. Return the pan to the oven and cook until the rice is crispy on top, the lentils or beans are very dry, and the mushrooms are deep brown—about 15 minutes. If your rice was very freshly cooked or put in the oven frozen, it may take an additional 10 to 15 minutes for the rice to dry out to this point. If this is the case, remove the mushrooms and lentils or beans from the pan when done and continue to cook the rice.

3 In the meantime, if you're using them, pulse the walnuts in a food processor until they are finely chopped. When the lentils or beans, mushrooms, and rice have finished roasting, add them to the food processor as well and process until finely chopped. Then add the flour, egg, barbecue sauce, salt, garlic powder, and rosemary (if desired) to the food processor. Process until the ingredients are well combined

CONTINUED . . .

. . . CONTINUED

and the mixture
pulls away from
the sides of the
bowl and starts
to form a loose
ball. If the mixture is
too dry and not coming
together, add more barbecue sauce.

4 Form the mixture by hand into five patties
(it will be a bit sticky). Heat the oil in a large
skillet over medium heat, then add the patties and cook until
they are golden brown and firm—about 4 minutes per side. You can
also drizzle the patties with oil and bake them on a baking sheet at
400°F for 20 minutes, flipping halfway through. Or grill them! If grilling, chill the uncooked
patties until they are firm, then brush them with olive oil before adding to the grill.

FREEZE IT

Freeze cooked patties for up to 5 months. To thaw, bake at 350°F for 12 to 15 minutes or microwave on high for 1 minute.

NOTE

Cooking ½ cup uncooked rice will give you the 1½ cups cooked rice the recipe calls for. You can also take a shortcut by using frozen or microwavable brown rice.

My favorite things to grow are tomatoes, peppers, and strawberries

sweet potato pierogies

When I was growing up in Western New York, there were always plenty of wings, beef on weck sandwiches—and pierogies! Pierogies are usually created by making a flour dough and filling it with mashed potatoes. They are simple but perfect . . . well, they are now that I've added sweet potato to the dough. These unbelievable little bites are chewy, slightly sweet, and totally addictive. I've never served these to anyone who hasn't gone nuts for them. Don't get me wrong, pierogies can be time-consuming to make, but make a ton and freeze them. I promise it's worth the effort.

— MAKES 18 PIEROGIES —

PIEROGI FILLING

1 large russet **potato** (12 ounces)

1 cup shredded cheddar cheese (4 ounces)

¼ cup sour cream

1 teaspoon kosher salt

¼ teaspoon ground black pepper

SWEET POTATO PIEROGIES

2 large **sweet potatoes** (18 ounces)

1¾ cups all-purpose flour + more as needed

1 large egg

1 teaspoon kosher salt

FOR SAUTÉING

3 tablespoons unsalted butter

1 tablespoon finely chopped scallions (green parts only)

Sour cream

Ground black pepper, for a garnish

TO MAKE THE FILLING:

1 Poke several holes in the potato with a fork. Cook it in the microwave on high until very soft—5 to 7 minutes. Alternatively, you can do this in the oven at 425°F for 50 to 60 minutes, but I do not do well waiting any longer than I need to for my pierogies.

2 Remove the potato from the microwave and allow it to cool slightly; once it is cool enough to handle, cut it in half and scoop the flesh into a medium bowl. Mash the potato with a fork or potato masher until it is smooth (this should give you about 1 cup mashed potato). Add the cheddar, sour cream, salt, and pepper and stir to combine all ingredients.

TO MAKE THE SWEET POTATO PIEROGIES:

1 Poke several holes in the sweet potatoes with a fork. Cook in the microwave on high until very soft—5 to 7 minutes. Alternatively, you can do this in the oven at 350°F for 1 hour.

2 Remove the sweet potatoes from the microwave and allow them to cool slightly; once they are cool enough to handle, cut them in half lengthwise and scoop the flesh into a medium bowl.

<u>BY HAND:</u> Mash the sweet potato flesh with a fork or potato masher until it is smooth (this should give you about 1¼ cups sweet potato puree), then add the flour, egg, and salt. Use your hands to mix the ingredients thoroughly to create a dough-like consistency. The dough should be workable and easy to

CONTINUED . . .

. . . CONTINUED

manipulate; add extra flour if it's too sticky. Form the dough into a ball and set it aside on a heavily floured work surface.

FOOD PROCESSOR: Scoop the sweet potato flesh directly into the food processor, rather than into a bowl. Process it until smooth, add the flour, egg, and salt, then process again until a smooth dough forms, adding flour as needed.

MIXER: To use a stand mixer, scoop the sweet potato flesh directly into the bowl of the mixer and use the mixer attachment to mash it. Add the flour, egg, and salt and switch out to the dough hook. Mix until a smooth dough forms, adding flour as needed.

3 Place a large pot of salted water over high heat for cooking the pierogies. On a heavily floured work surface, gently roll the dough into a flat sheet ⅛ to ¼ inch thick. Don't be afraid of flour—if anything is sticking, add more flour to your rolling pin and/or surface.

4 Using a 3½-inch-diameter ring mold, cut 18 rounds out of the dough. Don't have a ring mold? Try a widemouthed glass or the top of a mason jar lid, or just cut out some less perfect circles with a knife.

5 Scoop out 1 heaping tablespoon of the filling and roll it into an oval ball in your hand; it should look like a football. Place it in the center of one of the dough rounds and fold the round in half over the filling, squeezing the edges of the dough together; if you're having trouble getting the edges to stick together, brush them with a little water. Repeat this process with the remaining rounds, placing finished pierogies onto a heavily floured work surface or tray as you work.

6 Add the pierogies to the now-boiling water and cook until they are firm and floating—3 to 5 minutes. Drain the pierogies; if you are working in batches, set the cooked pierogies aside on an oiled surface.

7 To sauté, heat the butter in a large skillet over medium-high heat. Once the butter is hot, cook the pierogies in the pan in a single layer until they are golden brown—2 to 3 minutes on each side. Top with the scallions, a dollop of sour cream, and some pepper.

SERVING SUGGESTION

A great addition to the pierogies, along with the scallion and sour cream, is 3 ounces sautéed baby spinach and 1 cup caramelized onions.

FREEZE IT

After forming the pierogies in Step 5, place them, uncooked, on a floured sheet pan so that they are not touching, then place the entire sheet pan in the freezer until the pierogies are frozen solid. Once frozen, transfer them to a food storage bag and return to the freezer for up to 5 months. When you're ready to cook the pierogies, heat a large pot of salted water over high heat. Once the water is boiling, add the pierogies and cook them until they are warmed through—5 to 6 minutes. Then continue with Step 7.

walnut + mushroom meatloaf

We jokingly refer to my father-in-law Bob's meatloaf as an "onion loaf." The man loves his onions! Now, don't get me wrong, his onion loaf is pretty tasty and he really is onto something—meatloaf is a great dish for some veggie add-ins. I've still got the onions here, but I'm also bringing in mushrooms to enhance the beef flavor, walnuts for a subtle, nutty crunch, and oats to tie it all together. In the end, you can serve this meatloaf with veggies and a grain—or just eat it by itself since it's become an all-in-one meal.

SERVES 6 TO 8

1 cup raw walnuts (3 ounces)

8 ounces cremini **mushrooms**, sliced or whole

¾ cup quick oats

½ cup whole milk

2 tablespoons extra-virgin olive oil

1 medium yellow **onion** (8 ounces), finely chopped (1½ cups)

1 tablespoon chopped fresh thyme leaves

2 garlic cloves, minced

¼ cup + ¾ cup ketchup, divided

1 pound ground beef

1 large egg

2 teaspoons kosher salt

¼ teaspoon ground black pepper

1 Preheat the oven to 350°F and prepare a 9 × 5-inch loaf pan by spraying it heavily with cooking oil spray. Alternatively, to help lift the meatloaf out of the pan later, line the pan with parchment paper, leaving an overhang on each side.

2 Pulse the walnuts in a food processor until they are finely chopped, then transfer them to a small bowl and set aside. Pulse the mushrooms in the food processor until they are also finely chopped and set aside in another small bowl (the food processor makes this really easy, but you can also do the chopping in this step by hand with your knife; just keep going until everything's as finely chopped as possible).

3 In a large bowl, combine the oats and milk, then set aside. Heat the oil in a large sauté pan over medium-high heat, add the mushrooms and onion, and cook until the veggies are tender and lightly browned in spots—8 to 10 minutes. Add the thyme and garlic and continue cooking until fragrant—1 to 2 minutes.

4 Remove the pan from the heat and transfer the mixture to the bowl of soaked oats. Add the walnuts and ¼ cup of the ketchup and stir to combine.

5 Add the beef, egg, salt, and pepper. Use your hands to mix the ingredients together until they are well combined, trying not to overmix, then transfer the beef mixture to the prepared loaf pan, lightly pressing the mixture down into an even layer. Spread the remaining ¾ cup ketchup evenly on top.

6 Bake until the ketchup goes from shiny and glossy to matte and brown in spots and the meatloaf reaches an internal temperature of 160°F—1 hour to 1 hour 15 minutes. Remove the meatloaf from the oven and allow it to cool for 20 minutes before slicing and serving.

zucchini crust pizza

As my kids get older, they get more particular about their pizza. They want the real thing—a slice of zucchini covered in sauce and cheese just doesn't cut it anymore (oh, those were the days!). So I decided to pass off zucchini a different way by fortifying my favorite pizza dough with it.

Zucchini is a perfect addition. It's not too dense, so it allows the dough to rise and the glutens to develop, resulting in an airy, chewy crust. Dough can be intimidating, but I'm here to make it easy and then show you all my tips and tricks for cooking up restaurant-quality pizza at home (see How to Cook Pizza on page 158). Together we can do anything—and we can definitely make some great pizza.

—————— MAKES TWO 12-OUNCE DOUGH BALLS ——————

1 medium **zucchini** (9 ounces), chopped (2 cups)

One ¼-ounce packet instant or active dry yeast (2¼ teaspoons)

2 teaspoons granulated sugar

2¼ cups all-purpose flour + more as needed

1 teaspoon kosher salt

2 tablespoons olive oil + more for drizzling

1 Blend the zucchini and ¼ cup hot tap water in a blender until very smooth, then transfer to a medium microwave-safe bowl. Test the mixture with your finger; you want it to be the temperature of warm, but not scalding, bath water (105°F to 110°F). If it's too cold, microwave it in 10-second intervals until warm. Temperature is very important for getting the yeast to rise.

2 Stir the yeast and sugar into the zucchini-water mixture, allowing it to rest until it is foamy and has doubled in size—about 10 minutes. If the mixture does not become bubbly, your yeast may be expired or your zucchini water may have been too hot, so you will need to try again.

3 While the yeast activates, stir the flour and salt together in the bowl of a stand mixer. Once the yeast is activated, add the bubbly yeast mixture and the oil to the flour and salt and stir to combine until a loose dough forms. Your dough will be green but will become brown after cooking.

4 Using your mixer's dough attachment, knead the dough on medium-low, adding more flour as needed, until the dough is smooth and elastic and comes together in a loose ball—about 5 minutes. At this point, it's okay if the dough is a little sticky, but depending on how moist your zucchini was, you may need to add up to ½ cup more flour. Transfer the

CONTINUED . . .

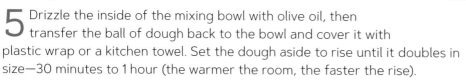

dough to a floured surface (no need
to clean out the bowl; you'll need it
in a minute) and knead it a couple of
times to form a ball. You can also do
this entire process by hand, kneading the
dough by hand for 5 to 7 minutes.

5 Drizzle the inside of the mixing bowl with olive oil, then
transfer the ball of dough back to the bowl and cover it with
plastic wrap or a kitchen towel. Set the dough aside to rise until it doubles in
size—30 minutes to 1 hour (the warmer the room, the faster the rise).

6 Once the dough has risen, transfer it to the floured surface, cut the ball in half,
then roll each half out to make pizza or store for later!

FREEZE IT + STORE IT

*You can make this dough and let it rise completely, divide it into two balls, then place each ball into
a separate freezer bag with the air gently squeezed out; freeze for up to 3 months. To thaw, leave
the dough on the countertop until you're ready to roll it out; it usually thaws completely in under
1 hour. Alternatively, you can store the dough in the fridge for up to 3 days; allow it to come to room
temperature before rolling.*

SWAP IT

Yellow squash works well as a sub for the zucchini.

how to cook pizza

The perfect pizza crust should be crispy and crunchy on the outside, while still being soft and delicate on the inside. Most methods dry out the crust too much or don't give you any crusty brown spots (always my favorite part). So here are three of the very best methods I could come up with for making stellar pizza at home. No fancy equipment or pizza ovens required!

Each of the cooking methods below uses one of the two 12-ounce balls of dough that the Zucchini Crust Pizza dough recipe (page 155) yields.

oven

The oven is always a great go-to for pizza, but if you simply put the dough on a pan, top, and bake, your results will be less than stellar. Try my method here for the very best way to cook a pizza in the oven without a pizza stone or special pan.

*

Preheat the oven to 500°F and position your oven rack as close to the top of the oven as possible while leaving space for the pizza. Roll the dough out to about a 10 × 14-inch oval and place it on a baking sheet. Drizzle the top of the dough with olive oil, use your hands to spread it around to the edges, then flip the dough, placing the oiled side down on the baking sheet. Brush the side that is now facing up with olive oil as well, spreading it to the edges. Prick the dough all over with a fork (but not on the crust edges) to prevent too much bubbling up, then bake until the top of the dough is golden brown—about 5 minutes. Remove from the oven, flip, and top as desired. Next, gently slide the half-cooked, topped pizza off the baking sheet and onto the oven rack itself; continue baking until the cheese is bubbly and brown and the crust is golden brown all over—about 5 minutes more.

grill

Let me start off by saying that each grill is different, so use these instructions as a starting point. If your crust ends up dried out, cook it a little hotter next time, and if it's getting burned or browns too fast, try a lower temp. Also, your toppings will not become as brown and cooked as they will with other cooking methods, so consider precooking things like sausage, peppers, and onion. Although there might be a slight learning curve, it's totally worth the effort. This is my favorite way to cook pizza at home.

*

Preheat the grill, setting the burners to medium. Roll the dough out to about a 10 × 14-inch oval and place it on a baking sheet (be sure it's a rimless baking sheet, if you don't have one, flip over your rimmed baking sheet and use the bottom side). Drizzle the top of the dough heavily with olive oil, use your hands to spread it around to the edges, then flip the dough, placing the oiled side down on the baking sheet. Carefully slide the pizza off the far side of the baking sheet and onto the grill, shaking it to get it off the baking sheet. Close the lid and cook until the bottom is crisp and has grill marks—2 to 8 minutes (the time depends largely on your specific grill, and the dough can burn easily, so keep an eye on it). Remove the dough from the grill and transfer it back to the baking sheet, flipping it so the cooked side is up. Top the dough as desired, then return the pizza to the grill, close the lid, and cook until the cheese is melted and the crust is crisp on the bottom—2 to 8 minutes more.

skillet

The skillet method is fun because it guarantees a crispy crust, as you are both baking in the oven and heating on the stovetop. The result is more of a deep-dish-style pizza, with a thicker crust.

*

Preheat the oven to 500°F and position the rack as close to the top of the oven as possible while leaving room for your pizza. Drizzle 2 tablespoons olive oil into a large cast-iron pan (not set over any heat yet), then spread the oil around the pan until the bottom is fully coated. Roll the dough out to the approximate size of your pan, then place the dough in the pan, pressing it to the sides; brush the outer crust edge with additional olive oil and top the dough as desired. Set the pan over high heat and cook the pizza until the crust is medium brown, one shade lighter than you want in the end—4 to 5 minutes. Transfer the half-baked pizza, still in the pan, to the oven and bake until the cheese is bubbly and brown and the crust is golden brown—4 to 5 minutes more. Remove the pizza from the pan, cut, serve, and enjoy!

MORE VEGGIES ON THE SIDE AND AT SNACK TIME

Sides and snacks deserve the same attention as main dishes, if not more. Sides are often where the fun happens at mealtime and allow you to serve up an array of colors, tastes, and textures. And when your kids are having a day where they are endlessly hungry, bring on the snacks! Snack time is a big deal in our house, and I get it, snacks are fun. And when you see how easy it is to amp up go-to snacks like crackers, applesauce, and chips with veggies, suddenly snack time is just as nutritious as dinner.

creamed spinach garlic bread

The sell here is simple: I combined creamed spinach and garlic bread for a truly magical result. This bread uses two bags of spinach combined with tangy Parm, garlic, and a hint of cream, all spread on top of crusty, chewy bread. Top it with melty mozzarella for some outrageous comfort food that's so nutritious you just might be having Creamed Spinach Garlic Bread every night this week. It's a favorite recipe in my house, and I'm sure it will be one of yours too.

--- MAKES 10 PIECES OF GARLIC BREAD ---

2 teaspoons olive oil

8 garlic cloves, sliced

10 cups **baby spinach** (10 ounces)

⅔ cup grated Parmesan cheese (3 ounces)

¼ cup heavy cream

1 teaspoon kosher salt

¼ teaspoon ground nutmeg

¼ teaspoon ground black pepper

1 loaf French or Italian bread, halved lengthwise + horizontally

1 cup shredded mozzarella cheese (4 ounces)

¼ teaspoon red pepper flakes (optional)

1 Preheat the broiler to high. In a large pot over medium heat, cook the oil and garlic until the garlic is fragrant and tender—about 5 minutes. Add the spinach and cook until it is wilted and most of the liquid is gone from the pan—5 to 7 minutes more.

2 Add the Parmesan and cream and cook until the cheese has melted—about 3 minutes. Add the salt, nutmeg, and ground black pepper, stir to combine, and remove from the heat.

3 While the creamed spinach cooks, place the bread cut-side-up on a baking sheet, then bake it (on a lower oven rack if possible) until it is dried out around the edges and lightly toasted—1 to 5 minutes, depending on your oven and type of bread. Remove from the oven and set aside.

4 Remove the spinach mixture from the heat and spread it on top of the cut side of the bread, spooning any remaining liquid in the pan over the top of the bread as well. Divide the mozzarella among the bread halves, then sprinkle with the red pepper flakes (if desired). Broil the bread on high (this time on a higher oven rack) until the cheese is melted and slightly brown—2 to 5 minutes. Cut and serve.

10 cups of baby spinach

1 pound
butternut
squash

butternut squash garlic rosemary focaccia

Focaccia is a staple found on many Italian tables, with an airy, flaky center and a crisp, crunchy exterior; you get the crunch by letting the dough sizzle in olive oil in the pan as it bakes. There's also olive oil *in* the dough, keeping the bread incredibly moist and rich.

In this recipe, things get really exciting because that oil is *garlic* infused and works alongside a whole pound of sweet butternut squash to weave this bread with incredible flavors. In short: it's incredibly delicious, simple as that.

─────────────── MAKES ONE 18 × 13-INCH LOAF OF BREAD ───────────────

1 cup + ¼ cup olive oil, divided

12 garlic cloves

One ¼-ounce packet instant or active dry yeast (2¼ teaspoons)

1 tablespoon granulated sugar

One 16-ounce bag frozen cubed **butternut squash** (about 4 cups)

5 cups all-purpose flour

1½ teaspoons kosher salt

2 tablespoons whole rosemary leaves

2 teaspoons sea salt or coarse kosher salt

1 In a small saucepan over medium-low heat, cook 1 cup of the oil along with the garlic (halve any extra-large cloves), stirring occasionally, until the garlic is tender and golden brown all over—about 15 minutes. Remove the pan from the heat, transfer the oil-garlic mixture to a bowl, and place it in the freezer to allow it to cool; you want the mixture to be warm or room temperature—not hot—when adding it to your dough later (otherwise you will kill your yeast).

2 While the garlic cooks, place ½ cup warm water in a medium bowl; the water should feel like warm, but not scalding, bath water (105°F to 110°F); temperature is very important for getting the yeast to rise correctly. Stir the yeast and sugar into the warm water, then allow the mixture to rest until it is foamy—about 10 minutes. If it doesn't get foamy, start over with new yeast.

3 While the yeast activates, microwave the frozen squash in a large bowl, stirring halfway through the cooking time, until it is fully thawed, warm, and tender—about 3 minutes. Blend the squash along with 1 cup water in a blender or food processor until the mixture is very smooth, then transfer it to the bowl of a stand mixer.

4 Also to the bowl of the stand mixer, add the flour, the cooled oil-garlic mixture (reserving 2 tablespoons of the oil for later use), the activated yeast mixture, and the 1½ teaspoons kosher salt. Using the dough hook attachment, mix

CONTINUED . . .

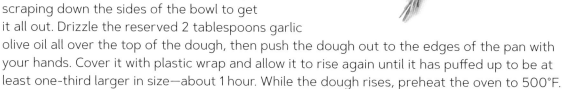

the ingredients together on low for 3 minutes, then increase the speed to medium for an additional 5 minutes. The dough will be very loose and wet, but have no fear—this is good. Remove the dough hook and cover the mixing bowl with a kitchen towel or plastic wrap, then set it aside to allow the dough to rise until it doubles in size—about 1 hour (the warmer the room, the faster the rise).

5 When the dough has risen, generously oil a rimmed baking sheet with the remaining ¼ cup olive oil. Pour the dough onto the pan, scraping down the sides of the bowl to get it all out. Drizzle the reserved 2 tablespoons garlic olive oil all over the top of the dough, then push the dough out to the edges of the pan with your hands. Cover it with plastic wrap and allow it to rise again until it has puffed up to be at least one-third larger in size—about 1 hour. While the dough rises, preheat the oven to 500°F.

6 Once the dough has risen, "punch" it all over with your fingertips to create dimples. Sprinkle the rosemary and sea salt (or coarse kosher salt) all over the dough. Bake the bread on the middle or lower rack of the oven until it is crisp and medium brown on top—13 to 20 minutes.

7 Remove the bread from the oven and allow it to cool in the pan for 5 minutes. Carefully remove it from the pan and transfer it to a wire cooling rack, then allow it to cool completely (you don't want to let it cool completely in the pan or the bottom will get soggy). Once the focaccia is completely cooled, slice it and serve. (If you cut it while it's hot, it will get super dried out; don't make the same mistake I did my first time.)

MAKE AHEAD

Form the dough on the baking sheet, then wrap it in plastic wrap. However, before allowing it to rise again, refrigerate it for up to 12 hours. When you're ready to bake, allow it to come to room temperature and rise again; this may take 1 to 2 hours. Once the dough has risen, resume with Step 6.

twice-baked potatoes

Roasting is an old, tried-and-true chef's trick. Basically, throw any raw veggie into a hot oven, give it a little time, and voilà! The veggie you pull out is beautifully browned with a toasty sweetness that wasn't there before.

When you roast, you caramelize the sugars in a veggie—yes, even veggies have sugar—giving your veggie a whole new flavor and texture. So adding roasted cauliflower to twice-baked potatoes just seemed like the right thing to do—that nutty cauliflower in those creamy, cheesy, bacony potato boats all drizzled with sour cream equals a side dish worthy of all the ahhhhhs and mmmmms.

MAKES 12 POTATOES

6 small russet **potatoes** (3 pounds)

1 medium head **cauliflower** (1½ pounds), stemmed + chopped (8 cups)

2 tablespoons olive oil

6 bacon strips

4 tablespoons unsalted butter

1 cup + 1 cup shredded cheddar cheese (8 ounces total), divided

¾ cup + 2 tablespoons whole milk, divided

½ cup + ¼ cup sour cream, divided

¼ cup grated Parmesan cheese (1 ounce)

½ teaspoon garlic powder

Kosher salt

Ground black pepper

1 scallion, finely chopped (green parts only), for a garnish

1 Preheat the oven to 425°F. On a baking sheet, toss the potatoes and cauliflower in the oil. Arrange the cauliflower on one half of the sheet and the potatoes on the other half. On a second baking sheet lined with parchment paper, arrange the bacon in a single layer. Place both baking sheets in the oven.

2 Bake the bacon until it is brown and crispy—about 15 minutes. Remove the bacon from the oven, leaving the baking sheet with the cauliflower and potatoes to continue baking. Transfer the bacon to a paper towel to drain and cool; once it is cool, chop it into small pieces and set aside.

3 Continue roasting the cauliflower until it is browned and tender—about 15 minutes more (30 minutes total cook time). Remove the baking sheet from the oven and transfer just the cauliflower to a medium bowl. Return the potatoes to the oven and continue roasting them until they are easily pierced with a fork— about 30 minutes

CONTINUED...

more (1 hour total cook time); set them aside and allow them to cool. Turn the oven down to 350°F.

4 Using a potato masher or fork, mash the cauliflower until it is mostly smooth. Alternatively, you can pulse it in a food processor until it is finely chopped. Once the potatoes are cool enough to touch, slice them in half lengthwise. Gently scoop out the flesh of the potatoes with a spoon, leaving less than ¼ inch of it inside the potato skins. Add the potato flesh along with the butter to the bowl with the cauliflower, then mash again until the mixture is mostly smooth and the butter has melted (do not mix the potatoes in the food processor if using, as it will make them gummy). Arrange the skins on the baking sheet cut-side-up.

5 Add 1 cup of the cheddar, ¾ cup of the milk, ½ cup of the sour cream, the Parmesan, garlic powder, and half of the chopped bacon to the bowl with the cauliflower and potatoes, and stir to combine all ingredients. Then stir in 1 teaspoon salt and ½ teaspoon pepper; taste the filling and add more salt and pepper if needed.

6 Spoon the filling into each of the potato skins. Sprinkle the potato halves with the remaining 1 cup cheddar and remaining chopped bacon. Bake until the potatoes are warmed through and the cheese is melted—about 10 minutes.

7 While the potatoes cook, whisk together the remaining ¼ cup sour cream and 2 tablespoons milk in a small bowl; you want a consistency that you can drizzle. Remove the potatoes from the oven and transfer them to a serving dish. Drizzle with the thinned sour cream, garnish with the scallion, and enjoy!

NOTE

You will end up with extra filling—that's just the nature of twice-baked potatoes. The filling can be enjoyed as a side dish for another meal or as an incredible filling for my Sweet Potato Pierogies (page 149).

FREEZE IT

These freeze great! You can freeze the assembled potatoes before baking and drizzling with sour cream, or freeze completely cooked and cooled twice-baked potatoes if you end up with leftovers. Whichever you choose, when you're ready to enjoy, bake the frozen potatoes at 350°F until warm throughout—about 45 minutes.

cauliflower inside

⅔ potatoes,
⅓ cauliflower

brown butter garlic mashed potatoes with cauliflower

Mashed potatoes might seem simple enough, but making *the best* mashed potatoes is a subtle art (that I will still make simple). Let's start with the potatoes themselves—Yukon Gold potatoes are the perfect base because of their incredibly creamy texture and taste. We'll cook the potatoes whole, which prevents them from becoming waterlogged and allows for a more intense potato flavor. And to bring the already amazing texture and flavor up another notch, let's fold in creamy, delicate cauliflower puree.

Now that you have a beautiful mash, bring on the butter! But not just any butter—brown butter! Browning toasts the milk solids in your butter, which transforms the average stick into a flavor powerhouse—the butter becomes intensely rich and nutty. Last but not least, let's cook the garlic in that brown butter to give it a roasted quality with no need for the oven. It all comes together easily and is ready for Thanksgiving—or Tuesday night, which can be pretty awesome too.

—— MAKES 8 CUPS ——

3 pounds medium Yukon Gold **potatoes** (9–12 total), peeled

1 medium head **cauliflower** (1½ pounds), coarsely chopped (8 cups)

½ cup unsalted butter (1 stick)

4 large garlic cloves, halved lengthwise

4 large sprigs fresh thyme

½ cup heavy cream

Kosher salt

Ground black pepper

1 Add the potatoes to a large pot of salted water, covering them by 2 inches, then bring to a low boil and cook for 15 minutes. Add the cauliflower and continue cooking until both the potatoes and cauliflower are easily pierced with a fork— about 15 minutes more. Drain the vegetables, reserving ½ cup of the cooking water. Set the potatoes in a large bowl and transfer the cauliflower to the bowl of a food processor.

2 Melt the butter in a small pot over medium heat. When it is just melted, add the garlic and thyme and continue to cook, stirring frequently, until the butter is browned and the garlic is tender—5 to 7 minutes. You'll know it's ready because the butter closest to the pan will turn medium to deep brown and smell nutty. Remove from the heat immediately to stop the butter and garlic from cooking, as they can burn easily. Remove the thyme sprigs and set them aside, but do not discard them. Pour the butter-garlic mixture into the food processor with the cauliflower, reserving 2 tablespoons of the brown butter for finishing.

CONTINUED . . .

3 Process the cauliflower and butter until the mixture is very smooth. Add the cream and process again until well incorporated.

4 Use a potato masher to smash the potatoes until they are mostly smooth. (For extra smooth and fluffy potatoes, you can put them through a food mill or ricer. Do not put potatoes in the food processor.) Add the cauliflower mixture, 2 teaspoons salt, and ½ teaspoon pepper to the bowl with the potatoes, and stir until all the ingredients are incorporated and the potatoes are smooth (if necessary, add the reserved cooking water, 2 tablespoons at a time, to loosen up the mixture). Taste the mashed potatoes and add more salt and pepper if needed.

5 To serve, transfer the mashed potatoes to a serving dish and drizzle them with the reserved brown butter. Pull some of the thyme leaves from the reserved sprigs and sprinkle them over the top of the potatoes; alternatively, you can place the whole sprig in the center of the dish as a garnish. Serve immediately.

SWAP IT

Chives can be subbed for the thyme. Simply leave the thyme out of the recipe and when the mashed potatoes are complete, stir in 2 tablespoons chopped chives; garnish with 1 tablespoon on top.

MAKE AHEAD

Before topping with the thyme and extra brown butter, let the mashed potatoes cool completely and refrigerate covered with foil for up to 5 days. To serve, cook the mashed potatoes (still covered with foil) in an oven heated to 375°F for 30 minutes; stir, cover again with foil, and continue cooking until hot throughout—about 15 minutes more. Remove and garnish.

garlic spinach naan

Naan is a flatbread found in many Asian and some Caribbean cuisines. It has become especially popular worldwide because of its role in Indian cooking. With this naan, I'm sticking with traditional ingredients like yogurt (to make it soft) and yeast (to make it chewy and give it some rise), but I'm also adding some new and very delicious elements—garlic and *spinach*. Oh, and I'm slathering it in garlic butter and adding a pop of salt that will knock your socks off. In the end, it's a special naan that does the original version proud while getting its own time in the spotlight.

—————————————— MAKES FOUR 7 × 9-INCH PIECES OF NAAN ——————————————

6 tablespoons unsalted butter

6 garlic cloves, minced

Kosher salt

3 cups **baby spinach** (3 ounces)

1 tablespoon granulated sugar

One ¼-ounce packet instant or active dry yeast (2¼ teaspoons)

2 cups all-purpose flour + more as needed

1 teaspoon garlic powder

¼ cup plain Greek yogurt (2 ounces)

Sea salt or coarse kosher salt, for sprinkling

1 Cook the butter, garlic, and a pinch of kosher salt in a small pot over medium heat until the garlic is tender and fragrant—about 5 minutes.

2 Process the spinach, ½ cup water, and 3 tablespoons of the garlic butter from Step 1 (trying to get a good combo of butter and garlic pieces) in a food processor until the mixture is very smooth, then transfer it to a medium microwave-safe bowl. Microwave in 10-second intervals until the mixture is just warm to the touch but is not as hot as a warm bath (105°F to 110°F), then stir to ensure the heat is distributed evenly. If it's too hot, let it cool down, as temperature is very important here.

3 Stir the sugar and yeast into the spinach-water mixture, then allow it to rest until it is foamy—about 10 minutes. If the mixture does not become bubbly and grow, your yeast may be expired or your spinach water may have been too hot, so you will need to try again.

4 While the yeast activates, whisk the flour, garlic powder, and 1 teaspoon kosher salt in a large bowl until combined. Add the yogurt and activated yeast mixture and stir with a spoon (not your hands) until a dough comes together

CONTINUED . . .

(it should be a little sticky). If the dough is too dry and not coming together and/or not sticky at all, add a splash of water; if the dough is extremely wet, add a touch more flour.

5 Leave the dough in the bowl and cover it with plastic wrap or a kitchen towel, then set it aside to rise until the dough doubles in size—about 1 hour. This may take longer if your room is cooler (the warmer the air, the faster the rise).

6 Once the dough has risen, turn the bowl upside down and allow the dough to fall onto a lightly floured surface, scraping if necessary to get it all out (it will be soft). Sprinkle the dough with more flour, but don't knead it. Cut the dough into quarters, then roll each piece out into a 7 × 9-inch oval about ⅛ inch thick (you need it thin or it won't cook properly), adding more flour to your surface and rolling pin as needed. Really any size or shape is fine, but if you want to keep your naan traditional, form it into a teardrop shape. I tend to roll and cook one piece of naan at a time, as the dough ovals are soft and can be difficult to move around.

7 Heat a large cast-iron or high-heat nonstick skillet (one with a lid, preferably glass so you can see the bread—see note), over high heat, giving it time to get really hot. Dust the excess flour off the dough oval, then cook it in the pan (no oil necessary), covered, until large bubbles form and it is charred in spots—1 to 1½ minutes; flip the dough and re-cover the pan. Cook the second side of the dough until it is charred in spots, but not burned—an additional 45 seconds to 1 minute. Remove the naan and slather it with some of the remaining garlic butter and a sprinkle of kosher salt (the coarser, the better) or sea salt. Then repeat Step 7 (wiping the excess flour from the pan as necessary) until all the ovals have been cooked, buttered, and salted.

FREEZE IT

Freeze naan (without the finishing butter and salt) for up to 5 months (you can even freeze the garlic butter on the side); to reheat, microwave for 15 to 20 seconds, or wrap a piece of naan in foil and bake at 350°F for 3 to 5 minutes, then top with butter and salt. Naan from the fridge is also best warmed before eating.

NOTE

If you don't have a lid to fit your pan, use another pan or a baking sheet to cover it as best you can. You want to create somewhat of a seal to keep some steam in the pan, which helps the naan puff up.

vegetable shapes

You might be looking at these and wondering, *Um, what is that?* Well, it's my side of veggies when I don't have time to cook up something fresh. It's a patty made of potato, carrot, and spinach, and it's just what you need in your fridge or freezer for a quick side when mealtime has snuck up on you, yet again. Man, these kids eat *all the time*! So make some shapes, freeze 'em up along with my Chicken Nuggets (page 74), and have a super nutritious meal straight from the freezer.

MAKES 25 SHAPES

1 large russet **potato** (12 ounces)

1 medium **carrot** (2½ ounces), chopped (½ cup)

One 10-ounce package frozen chopped **spinach**, thawed

½ cup **wheat germ**

½ cup grated Parmesan cheese (2 ounces)

1 large egg, beaten

1 teaspoon garlic powder

1 teaspoon kosher salt

¼ teaspoon ground black pepper

All-purpose flour, for dusting

2 tablespoons olive oil + more as needed

1 Add the potato to a large pot of salted water, covering it by 1 inch, then bring to a low boil and cook for 15 minutes. Add the carrot and continue cooking until both the potato and carrot are easily pierced with a fork—about 20 minutes more; then drain well and allow to cool slightly.

2 While the potato and carrot cook, transfer the thawed spinach to a kitchen towel; roll up the cloth and twist and squeeze out as much liquid as you can (alternatively, you can push the spinach into a mesh strainer to remove the liquid). You want to get all the excess moisture out to ensure you won't have soggy nuggets.

3 When the potato is cool enough to handle, peel it (the skin should come off easily with the back of a butter knife or spoon) and transfer it to a large bowl along with the carrot. Use a potato masher or fork to coarsely mash the vegetables (small lumps are fine and are actually desired for these nuggets). Add the spinach, wheat germ, Parmesan, egg, garlic powder, salt, and pepper and stir until the mixture is very well combined.

4 Transfer the mixture to a cutting surface heavily dusted with flour; dust the top of the mixture with flour, then pat it into a ½-inch-thick square (the mixture will be a little loose). Using a knife, firmly cut down (hard enough to cut through the spinach) on the mixture to create 2-inch squares, then cut some of the squares in half to create triangles. If the mixture sticks to your surface, don't stress—just work it back together, adding more flour to the surface, and try again; a little extra flour in the mixture will not hurt it. You can also skip the rolling and cutting and press some of the mixture into a small ring mold to make circles (using a ring mold or cookie cutter to stamp out shapes doesn't work, as it won't cut through the spinach).

5 Heat the oil in a large pan over medium-high heat. Add the nuggets, working in batches and adding additional oil if necessary; cook them until both sides are golden brown, flipping them halfway through—4 to 6 minutes per side. Transfer the cooked nuggets to paper towels to absorb any excess oil. Alternatively, if you prefer, you can bake your nuggets at 400°F for 15 to 20 minutes, flipping halfway through the cooking time.

FREEZE IT

Freeze cooked and cooled vegetable shapes in a plastic storage bag for up to 5 months. To thaw, place the frozen shapes onto a greased baking sheet and bake at 400°F, flipping halfway through the cooking time, until the nuggets are lightly crispy and hot throughout—about 15 minutes.

SWAP IT

Sub ½ cup regular breadcrumbs for the wheat germ if you don't have any on hand.

buffalo cauliflower wings

I'm sure you serious wing aficionados think replacing the chicken with a vegetable is blasphemy. But as a Buffalo gal who can devour a plate of wings with the best of them, I'm telling you—these are insanely good. The Buffalo sauce is on point, and broiling the "wings" adds a bit of smokiness and char. Although it's not chicken, it is doing the wing proud. I promise you these will fly off the platter. Man, I just made myself really hungry writing this. I gotta go make some cauliflower wings!

——————— MAKES 35 CAULIFLOWER WINGS ———————

BUFFALO WING SAUCE

6 tablespoons unsalted butter

½ cup Frank's RedHot Original Cayenne Pepper Sauce

1 tablespoon distilled white vinegar

1 tablespoon packed brown sugar

Kosher salt (optional)

BUFFALO CAULIFLOWER WINGS

1½ cups all-purpose flour + more as needed

1 cup whole milk + more as needed

2 tablespoons Frank's RedHot Original Cayenne Pepper Sauce

1 tablespoon Worcestershire sauce

1 teaspoon kosher salt

1 teaspoon garlic powder

¼ teaspoon ground black pepper

1 medium head **cauliflower** (1½ pounds), broken into florets (6 cups)

Blue cheese, for serving

Celery, for serving

TO MAKE THE SAUCE:

In a small pot over medium-high heat, melt the butter. Whisk in the hot sauce, vinegar, and brown sugar until well combined. Remove the sauce from the heat, taste, add a pinch of salt if desired, then set aside (you can make this sauce while the cauliflower bakes during Step 2).

TO MAKE THE WINGS:

1 Preheat the oven to 475°F. Line two rimmed baking sheets with parchment paper and spray the parchment with cooking oil spray; make sure the parchment doesn't extend outside the baking sheet (later when you broil, you don't want it to burn).

2 In a large bowl, whisk together the flour, milk, hot sauce, Worcestershire sauce, salt, garlic powder, and pepper. The batter should be like a thick pancake batter. If it's too thick, add up to ¼ cup more milk to get the right consistency; if it's too thin, a touch more flour will thicken it up. Add the cauliflower to the bowl, tossing it in the mixture; shake off any excess, then spread it evenly between the two baking sheets. Bake the cauliflower until it is slightly browned in spots—about 20 minutes.

CONTINUED . . .

step 2

step 4

. . . CONTINUED

3 Once the cauliflower is browned, remove it from the oven and transfer it to a second large bowl. Add the Buffalo Wing Sauce and toss until all the cauliflower is coated in the sauce.

4 Preheat the broiler to high and scoop the cauliflower from the bowl back onto the baking sheets, leaving the excess sauce in the bowl; don't clean it yet. Working one baking sheet at a time, broil the cauliflower under the broiler until it is crispy and browned in spots—2 to 3 minutes more. Remove the broiled cauliflower wings from the oven and add them back to the bowl you used to toss them with the Buffalo Wing Sauce or brush them with the excess sauce from the bowl. Toss one last time to coat them with any remaining sauce, then serve with blue cheese and celery.

FREEZE IT

Freeze the completed wings in a single layer (not touching) on a baking sheet lined with foil. Once the wings are frozen, transfer them to a food storage bag and return to the freezer. To reheat, bake the wings at 375°F on a cooking oil–sprayed baking sheet until they are warmed through—10 to 15 minutes.

loaded queso

When I put queso out at a party, it's always the first thing to disappear. Who doesn't love hot, gooey cheese mixed with spicy salsa? I add some butternut squash for a subtle sweetness that balances out the heat, then top it with beans and all the fixings. It's got enough texture and flavor to almost be considered an entrée . . . at least for *this* cheese lover. Serve with chips or warm soft pretzels, use it to top your enchiladas—or just grab a spoon!

MAKES 3½ CUPS

1 tablespoon + 2 tablespoons unsalted butter, divided

½ small yellow onion (3 ounces), coarsely chopped (½ cup)

2 garlic cloves, sliced

Kosher salt

One 10-ounce bag frozen cubed **butternut squash** (2½ cups; see note)

1 cup chicken stock

½ teaspoon ground cumin

4 ounces cream cheese, cut into 1-inch pieces

2 tablespoons all-purpose flour

1 cup shredded mild cheddar cheese (4 ounces)

1 cup shredded Monterey Jack cheese (4 ounces)

¼ cup jarred salsa

TOPPINGS

½ cup canned **black beans** (3 ounces), drained, rinsed + warmed

¼ cup sour cream

2 tablespoons jarred salsa

2 tablespoons chopped scallions

1 Heat 1 tablespoon of the butter in a medium saucepan over medium heat. Add the onion, garlic, and ¼ teaspoon salt and sauté until the veggies are tender—about 5 minutes. Stir in the squash (no need to thaw) and continue to cook until the squash is thawed and easily squished with a spoon and the liquid at the bottom of the pan has evaporated— about 5 minutes. Transfer the veggies to a blender (no need to clean out the pot) along with the chicken stock, cumin, and another ¼ teaspoon salt, then blend until very smooth, letting the blender run to really break down the veggies. Add the cream cheese and blend again until completely smooth.

2 Melt the remaining 2 tablespoons butter in the empty veggie pot over medium

CONTINUED . . .

heat, then add the flour and whisk until the ingredients are well combined and completely smooth (a whisk really is necessary for this step and the next). Let the mixture cook for 2 minutes.

3 Slowly add the pureed butternut squash mixture to the butter and flour, whisking continuously as you pour; continue whisking until the mixture is smooth. Cook, whisking frequently, until the mixture just starts to bubble and thicken—2 to 4 minutes.

4 Reduce the heat to low and stir in the cheddar and Monterey Jack a handful at a time, whisking constantly and allowing each handful of cheese to fully melt before adding another. Once all the cheese is melted, stir in the ¼ cup salsa. Taste the queso and add more salt if needed. The queso will be thick, but you can thin it out with a touch of additional chicken stock or water if desired.

5 Transfer the queso to a large serving bowl and top it with the black beans, then add the sour cream and the 2 tablespoons salsa. Garnish with the scallions and serve hot with your choice of dippers (my Garlic Lime Tortilla Chips on page 186 are great with it!).

NOTE

If you can't find frozen butternut squash, you can cut up 2½ cups fresh squash (10 ounces) and steam or boil it until it is very tender, then add it as you would the frozen squash.

SWAP IT

Look for an 8-ounce package of a blend of shredded cheddar and Monterey Jack—that's perfect for this recipe. You can also replace the Monterey Jack with more cheddar or pepper jack.

HACK IT

Thaw a 10-ounce package of cubed, frozen butternut squash, then puree it in a blender (do not squeeze out the liquid). Meanwhile, heat a 15-ounce jar of store-bought queso in a saucepan over medium heat. Stir the squash puree into the queso and continue to heat the mixture until it begins to bubble—about 3 minutes. Top and garnish as described in Step 5, then serve.

FREEZE IT

You can freeze the queso for up to 3 months. To thaw, cook it along with a splash of water in a covered pot over medium-low heat, stirring frequently until hot, melty, and irresistible.

butternut
squash

kale chips

Carrots, sweet potatoes, or beets transformed into homemade salty-but-healthy veggie chips instead of store-bought bagged chips! Sounds great, right? And that's how the internet gets you, proclaiming it's just that easy—which it's not. After suffering many failed veggie chip attempts and being on rocky terms with Pinterest, I now make only one kind. Kale chips! These take a mere 20 minutes, come out perfectly every time, and don't require any chopping or special equipment. And my kids are eating kale. Kale, I tell you!

MAKES 4 CUPS

1 bunch **kale** (about 10 large stalks; 10–12 ounces)

2 tablespoons apple cider vinegar

1 tablespoon olive oil

½ teaspoon garlic powder

¼ teaspoon onion powder

¼ teaspoon kosher salt

1 Preheat the oven to 275°F. Line two baking sheets with parchment paper (this is essential, so don't skip it!).

2 Remove the kale from the stems and tear the leaves into 3-inch-wide strips (it's okay to have some smaller pieces as well); this should give you about 10 cups (6 ounces) lightly packed kale. In a large bowl, whisk together the apple cider vinegar, oil, garlic powder, onion powder, and salt. Add the kale to the bowl and mix well using your hands; rub each of the kale leaves between your palms to evenly coat it with the oil and spices. After being coated, the leaves will appear shiny on all sides and will be brighter green in color.

3 Divide the coated kale evenly between the baking sheets, so that the leaves are lying flat and none of them overlap; don't crowd the pan. (If you have a few extra that don't fit, eat them. With the oil and spices, they are also great raw.) Bake the kale, rotating the pans halfway through the baking time, until the leaves are completely dried out but not brown—about 20 minutes. It may take an additional 5 to 7 minutes to reach complete crispiness, but at this point, continue checking the chips constantly, as they can go from perfectly dried out to brown and bitter very quickly.

4 Remove the kale chips from the oven and cool completely on the baking sheets. Eat immediately or store in brown paper bags on the countertop for up to 5 days.

NOTE
Baby kale does not work well for this recipe.

garlic lime tortilla chips

Homemade chips are pretty fun. You simply cut up corn tortillas, bake them, and olé—crunchy fun at your fingertips! But to make them special and truly something you will choose over the store-bought brand, they need to have *flavor*. These chips will dance on your tongue because of a special technique involving dehydrating lime zest in the microwave. Mix that zest with paprika, garlic powder, and salt and it makes for a spice mix like no other. It will feel like Cinco de Mayo no matter what time of year, and you'll have a great excuse to break out the margaritas.

— MAKES 40 CHIPS —

Ten 6-inch corn tortillas
Zest of 2 limes (see note)
1 teaspoon paprika
½ teaspoon kosher salt
½ teaspoon garlic powder

1 Preheat the oven to 325°F. Spray two baking sheets with cooking oil spray.

2 Stack the tortillas and cut them into fourths. Divide the cut tortillas between the baking sheets in single layers, then spray them evenly on both sides with cooking oil spray. Bake the tortillas until they are crispy and slightly golden brown—15 to 18 minutes. They harden as they cool, so if they seem a little soft when first removing them from the oven, don't worry, as they will likely crisp up.

3 While the chips cook, spread out the lime zest on a microwave-safe plate and microwave on high for 1 minute. Remove the zest from the microwave and stir it, then microwave it again until it is completely dried out—30 seconds more (if the zest is not completely dried out at this point, continue to microwave it at 15-second intervals until it is totally dry).

4 Into a small bowl, rub the dried zest between your fingers to grind it into a fine powder. Add the paprika, salt, and garlic powder and mix well. You can also use a spice grinder or a mortar and pestle to combine.

5 When the tortilla chips are finished baking, place the hot chips immediately into a brown paper bag and quickly wipe any excess oil from the baking sheets with a paper towel. Sprinkle half of the seasoning mix over the chips in the bag, then shake to distribute the mix over all the chips. Add the remaining half of the seasoning blend to the bag, shake again, then pour the chips back onto the wiped baking sheets to cool completely. Serve immediately or store in the paper bag at room temperature—they will stay crispy and fresh for about a week.

NOTE

Fresh limes work best for this and give you the most zing. In addition to the lime zest, you can also squeeze some lime juice over the chips right before serving.

SWAP IT

Make my Sweet Potato Tortillas (page 88) or my Yellow Squash Corn Tortillas (page 85) into chips rather than using store-bought corn tortillas. To do so, follow the recipe above but adjust the baking slightly; cook the Sweet Potato Tortillas at 325°F for 15 to 18 minutes and the Yellow Squash Corn Tortillas at 300°F for 20 to 25 minutes.

HACK IT

Instead of making your own chips, bake 40 store-bought tortilla chips (like Tostitos) on a baking sheet at 350°F for 3 minutes until warm (warming them allows the seasoning to stick), then toss/ shake the warm chips with the seasoning blend in a bag until well coated.

peas

pea guacamole

Before I started making this recipe, I often bought guacamole at the store. The twins *loved* it, and I loved giving it to them (all those healthy fats—perfect for growing people). And although the store-bought guac worked for us, when I began adding peas to my homemade version, and then perfected the ratios of onion, lime, and fresh cilantro, I created something that was definitely not available at the grocery store. The peas blend in perfectly, adding a touch of sweetness and perfectly playing a supporting role to the avocados. And considering none of my kids will touch peas on their own, this guac is a big win. The best part is I can have this on hand both for kid-approved lunches and as the perfect snack to accompany Mama's post-bedtime margaritas. Cheers!

— MAKES 2 CUPS —

2 large **avocados**
   (1¼ pounds)
1 cup frozen **peas**
   (5 ounces), thawed
Juice of 1 lime
   (2 tablespoons)
1 tablespoon olive oil
1 large garlic clove, finely
   grated
Kosher salt
1 plum tomato, chopped
   (½ cup)
¼ cup chopped cilantro +
   more for a garnish
¼ small red onion, finely
   minced (¼ cup)
1 small jalapeño, seeds + ribs
   removed, finely minced
   (3 tablespoons; optional)
Tortilla chips, for serving

1 Cut the avocados in half, remove the pits, and use a soupspoon to scoop their flesh into a medium bowl. Add the peas, lime juice, oil, garlic, and ¾ teaspoon salt, then mash with a fork until the ingredients are well combined and mostly smooth. Alternatively, for a smoother guacamole with no visible peas (as pictured), blend the above ingredients in a food processor.

2 Stir in the tomato, cilantro, onion, and jalapeño (if desired), then taste and add more salt and lime juice if needed. Transfer the guacamole to a serving bowl and garnish it with additional cilantro. Serve immediately with plenty of tortilla chips for dipping.

tofu ranch dressing

My kids always like a little "dippy-dippy." A dollop of ranch and suddenly veggies, meatballs, and even strawberries are gone in an instant (the strawberries and ranch is more of an acquired taste). So how do we improve upon this magic little sauce? Add some tofu, of course! Creamy tofu is the perfect textural base and brings in major protein. This will also take you only about 5 minutes to make. Fast, easy, *and* more nutritious? Bring on the dippy-dippy!

─────────────── MAKES 2 CUPS ───────────────

8 ounces **silken tofu**, drained (half of a 16-ounce package; see notes)

¼ cup mayonnaise

¼ cup full-fat plain Greek yogurt (2 ounces)

Juice of ½ lemon (1 tablespoon)

1 tablespoon distilled white vinegar

1 teaspoon kosher salt

½ teaspoon garlic powder

½ teaspoon onion powder

⅛ teaspoon ground black pepper

2 tablespoons chopped fresh chives or scallions (green parts only)

1 tablespoon chopped fresh dill (optional)

Process the tofu, mayonnaise, yogurt, lemon juice, vinegar, salt, garlic powder, onion powder, and pepper in the bowl of a food processor or blender until completely smooth, then transfer the mixture to a serving bowl. Stir in the chives or scallions and dill (if desired). Taste and add more seasonings or herbs if you like—it's your ranch, make it your way!—then enjoy with your favorite dipping snacks (no judgment here if you choose strawberries).

NOTES

* You can use other firmness grades of tofu (firm, extra-firm, etc.); this results in a thicker sauce that you can thin with water, if desired, and a very slight graininess that most people don't mind. Also, if you use a different firmness and your blender has a wide base, you may need to use the food processor, as there won't be enough liquid to get your blender blades moving.

* Got a leftover half package of tofu you don't know what to do with? Freeze for next time (yes, it freezes great!), then thaw before making this recipe.

HACK IT

In a blender, combine 16 ounces silken tofu (the full package, drained), ½ cup mayo, ½ cup Greek yogurt, 2 tablespoons distilled white vinegar, and one 1-ounce packet of ranch seasoning. Blend until smooth.

FREEZE IT

You can freeze the completed tofu ranch dressing for up to 3 months; thaw by refrigerating overnight. It tastes just like it was freshly made.

ranch pimento cheese spread

Believe it or not, pimento cheese has a pretty rich history. Let's take a trip back to the early 1900s when the two coolest ingredients to have in your kitchen were cream cheese, newly invented by Northern farmers, and jarred pimento peppers imported from Spain. One day you're sitting around in your hoopskirt reading a *Good Housekeeping* recipe that— gasp!—*combines the two*. Then, one hundred years after that, some crazy person (who, me?!) decides to throw beans, carrots, and some ranch seasoning into that combo, and guess what? . . . it's even better!

This innovative recipe for the new and improved pimento cheese makes quite a bit of spread, so feel free to use the extra to start slinging up grilled pimento cheese sandwiches (a favorite in my house). There will be as many "yums" as there were in 1908 when those geniuses first taste-tested their pimento cheese invention—actually, there will be more!

— MAKES 4 CUPS —

One 15-ounce can **cannellini beans**, drained + rinsed

8 ounces cream cheese, room temperature

1 cup + 1 cup shredded sharp cheddar cheese (8 ounces total), divided

1 medium **carrot** (2½ ounces), shredded (½ cup)

One 1-ounce packet ranch seasoning

One 4-ounce jar diced **pimentos**, drained

1 Process the cannellini beans in the bowl of a food processor until they are broken down and crumbly. Add the cream cheese, 1 cup of the cheddar, the carrot, and the ranch seasoning and blend until mostly smooth.

2 Transfer the mixture to a medium bowl and stir in the remaining 1 cup cheddar and the pimentos.

SERVING SUGGESTIONS

Enjoy as a dip or use to top my Mushroom + Onion Burgers (page 144), spread onto my Ham + Cheese Wraps in Homemade Spinach Tortillas (page 79), or layer into my Creamed Spinach Garlic Bread (page 162).

SWAP IT

No pimentos? No problem! They can easily be replaced with ½ cup chopped roasted red bell peppers, lightly sautéed red peppers, or raw red peppers.

oat + cheddar cheese crackers

Although cheese and carbs are the ultimate duo (and were the *only* two food groups on the Picky Nikki Food Pyramid), they don't offer a ton of nutritional value. Well, times have changed—enter these Cheez-It-inspired crackers with their salty, cheesy bite and crispy crunch that provide your body with so much more. Oats, wheat germ, and even carrot juice help make this snack both irresistible *and* good for you. It's the kind of cracker that feeds the Picky Nikki side of myself while making the Mama Nikki side feel good about the endless number of crackers devoured in this house.

MAKES 40 CRACKERS

⅔ cup all-purpose flour

½ cup old-fashioned rolled oats

¼ cup **wheat germ**

½ teaspoon kosher salt

¼ teaspoon baking powder

1 cup shredded sharp cheddar cheese (4 ounces)

2 tablespoons cold unsalted butter, cut into small pieces

¼ cup cold **carrot juice**

1 large egg, white + yolk separated

1 Preheat the oven to 325°F and line two baking sheets with parchment paper. In the bowl of a food processor, combine the flour, oats, wheat germ, salt, and baking powder, blending until the oats and wheat germ are very finely ground.

2 Add the cheddar and butter and pulse until a coarse meal forms (about 5 pulses). Add the carrot juice and egg white and continue to pulse until a crumbly dough forms; it will not be a smooth dough or come together in a big ball, but should come together nicely when squeezed in your hand.

3 On a lightly floured work surface, gently knead the dough to bring it together, then divide it into two pieces. Roll out one piece of the dough a touch thinner than ⅛ inch thick, almost as thin as you can make it. Dust the work surface, dough, and rolling pin with additional flour as needed; I also usually flip the dough a couple of times to ensure it is floured enough and does not get stuck to the counter. Cut the dough into 2-inch squares and transfer them to one of the baking sheets; they will not spread, so you don't need to leave a lot of space between them. Repeat this process with the second piece of dough.

4 Use a toothpick to dot each cracker in the center, making the "dot" bigger by moving the toothpick in a circle. Alternatively, you can prick each cracker randomly a couple of times with the toothpick, which is a little

faster—but less cute. In a small bowl, whisk together the egg yolk and 2 teaspoons water, then brush this mixture on top of each cracker.

5 Bake in the oven for 15 minutes, then rotate the baking sheets (you want these to cook evenly) and continue baking until the crackers are deep golden brown and crispy (they will crisp more as they cool)—10 to 12 minutes more. Allow the crackers to cool completely on the baking sheets before serving or storing.

STORE IT

Store completely cooled crackers in an airtight container at room temperature for up to a week.

SWAP IT

You can replace the wheat germ with ¼ cup whole wheat flour or ¼ cup more oats if desired. If you don't have carrot juice on hand, feel free to use water instead.

NOTE

For an extra nutritional kick, I like to add a sprinkle of chia seeds to the crackers after brushing with the egg wash and before baking.

parmesan spinach crackers

When Ivy wants a snack, it's gotta be crackers. When my twins started saying "mama" and "dada," "cracker" came shortly after. So with the number of boxes we go through, I made it a goal to cook up some better-for-you crackers.

However, crackers can be tricky to make and even harder to add veggies to. So what's my secret? I dry baby spinach out in the oven and process it into a flourlike consistency, guaranteeing a crispy, never-soggy cracker complete with tons of green goodness. I also add other healthy ingredients like whole wheat flour and chia seeds, finishing things off with nutty Parm and Italian seasoning on top. These perfectly crunchy crackers with their big spinach bite will be enjoyed not only by your snack-obsessed kids but also by dinner party guests, although my stash always tends to mysteriously go missing well before guests arrive.

—————— **MAKES 60 CRACKERS** ——————

3 cups **baby spinach** (3 ounces)

½ cup (2 ounces) + 2 tablespoons grated Parmesan cheese, divided

½ cup whole wheat flour

½ cup all-purpose flour

½ teaspoon kosher salt

4 tablespoons cold unsalted butter, cut into small cubes

1 teaspoon + 1 teaspoon **chia seeds**, divided

¼ cup milk

2 teaspoons Italian seasoning

1 large egg yolk

1 Preheat the oven to 275°F. Set a cooling rack inside a large baking sheet, then spread the spinach in a single layer on the cooling rack (some overlap is fine, but try to spread it out as much as possible).

2 Bake the spinach until it is dried out and crispy, but has not yet begun to brown—about 35 minutes. Remove the spinach from the oven and allow it to cool completely (cooling doesn't take long). Line two baking sheets with parchment paper and set them aside; increase the oven temperature to 350°F.

3 Once the spinach has cooled, transfer it to the bowl of a food processor and blend until it is finely ground. Add ½ cup of the Parmesan, the whole wheat flour, all-purpose flour, and salt, blending until well combined; allow the food processor to run for 1 minute to really finely grind everything. Add the butter and pulse until a coarse meal forms, then add 1 teaspoon of the chia seeds, pulsing just a couple of times to combine. Finally, add the milk and pulse until the mixture forms moist crumbles that hold together when you squeeze them in the palm of your hand (don't worry that it's not quite a cohesive dough; it will come together when you knead it in the next step).

4 Knead the mixture several times on a lightly floured surface until it forms a mostly smooth dough (it might still be a little crumbly, which is okay), then divide the dough into two equal pieces.

5 Roll out one piece of the dough a touch thinner than ⅛ inch thick (you want to roll it almost as thin as you can get it), dusting the surface, dough, and rolling pin with additional flour as needed. Use a 1½-inch round cutter to cut rounds of the dough (really, any size or shape will work if you prefer something different; you can also cut the dough into squares with your knife). Reroll the dough scraps as needed until the dough is used up, giving you about 30 rounds total. Transfer the cut rounds to one of the baking sheets (they won't spread, so you can put them relatively close together), then repeat this entire step with the second piece of dough.

6 With the tines of a fork, poke the centers of each cracker, creating a few tiny holes in them (so they don't puff up too much). In a small bowl, combine the remaining 2 tablespoons Parmesan, Italian seasoning, and remaining 1 teaspoon chia seeds, then set aside. In a second small bowl, whisk the egg yolk with 2 teaspoons water, then brush on top of each cracker. Last, sprinkle the Parmesan mixture evenly over the crackers.

7 Bake for 10 minutes, then reduce the temperature to 325°F and rotate the baking sheets. Continue to bake until the crackers are lightly browned and crispy—10 to 15 minutes more. Allow them to cool completely on the baking sheets before serving.

SWAP IT

* *When my kids were extra little, they preferred these with no Parm or Italian seasoning on top. So for more delicate palates, consider topping some with just chia seeds or simply brushing with the egg wash and leaving off additional toppings.*

* *If you don't have whole wheat flour, you can replace it with additional all-purpose flour (this means you'll use 1 cup AP flour total for the recipe).*

buffalo party mix

My in-laws love a good happy hour. They are the first ones to break out the good cheese, open a new flavor of potato chips, and blend up some margaritas. So when these happy hour pros went nuts for this Chex mix, I knew I was onto something. The flavor punch for this mix comes from carrot juice and hot sauce—Frank's, of course (#BuffaloGal). This combo gives you a salty, sweet, spicy bite that's certifiably addictive and perfect for outdoor summer happy hours and late-night snacking alike.

─────── MAKES 11 CUPS ───────

½ cup unsalted butter (1 stick)

⅓ cup Frank's RedHot Original Cayenne Pepper Sauce (see note)

⅓ cup **carrot juice**

2 teaspoons onion powder

2 teaspoons garlic powder

1½ teaspoons kosher salt

3 cups Wheat Chex cereal (5 ounces)

3 cups Corn Chex cereal (3 ounces)

2 cups veggie goldfish crackers, such as Pepperidge Farm brand (4 ounces)

2 cups small pretzels (3 ounces)

1½ cups salted roasted **chickpeas** (10 ounces)

1 Preheat the oven to 275°F. Prepare two large baking sheets with parchment paper. Melt the butter in a small saucepan over medium heat—3 to 4 minutes. Add the hot sauce, carrot juice, onion powder, garlic powder, and salt and whisk to combine.

2 In a large bowl, combine the Wheat Chex cereal, Corn Chex cereal, veggie goldfish crackers, pretzels, and roasted chickpeas. Drizzle half of the hot sauce mixture on the outer edge of the Chex mix on the inside of the bowl, then gently stir it in until it is mostly incorporated. Repeat this with the remaining hot sauce mixture until all the dry ingredients are coated. The goal of pouring the sauce on the bowl instead of directly on the mixture is to evenly spread the sauce onto everything instead of having a couple of the cereal squares soak up all the goodness.

3 Divide the mixture between the two prepared baking sheets, spreading it evenly in a single layer. Bake until the mix is dry and most of the cereal pieces are crispy (they will continue to crisp as they cool), stirring gently every 20 minutes or so—your total cook time could be anywhere from 40 minutes to 1 hour 20 minutes; this can vary a lot, so just keep checking.

4 Allow the mixture to cool completely on the baking sheets before serving.

NOTE

Not afraid of some kick? Add more Frank's RedHot Original Cayenne Pepper Sauce to the recipe—an additional ¼ cup should do the trick.

carrot juice

butternut squash applesauce

I remember being a kid and watching my friend's mom whip up some applesauce. I was in awe. It had never occurred to me that you could make applesauce yourself instead of buying it from the store. When approaching this recipe as an adult, I was reminded just how easy it actually is. Basically, you are just cooking down some apples and pureeing them. And just as easily, you can add some butternut squash to the pot, which I always have a bag of in the freezer. In the end, you've got a more nutritionally dense applesauce—while your apples still take center stage as the stars.

— MAKES 1½ CUPS —

4 apples, such as Gala or Honeycrisp (1½ pounds), peeled, cored + chopped (4 cups)

1 cup peeled + cubed **butternut squash** (4 ounces), fresh or frozen

½ teaspoon kosher salt

⅓ cup sugar or ¼ cup honey + more as needed (optional)

¼ teaspoon ground cinnamon (optional)

1 In a medium pot, bring the apples, 1½ cups water, squash, and salt to a boil. Lower the heat and simmer uncovered, stirring occasionally, until the apples and squash are very tender, adding more water if needed—25 to 45 minutes. Your cook time will depend on how big the pieces of apple and squash are, and if the squash was frozen or fresh. Just keep cooking until the apples and squash can be mushed with your spoon, and add a splash more of water if needed.

2 Turn off the heat and use an immersion blender, food processor, or blender to puree the mixture until it is smooth. Taste your applesauce and decide if you want to add the sugar or honey; this decision depends mainly on how sweet your apples are along with your personal preference (some people prefer no additional sugar, but I usually add some). Add the sugar or honey directly to the blender, food processor, or pot and blend again until the sugar or honey dissolves into the hot applesauce—about 20 seconds. At this point, add your cinnamon if desired.

3 Taste the applesauce and season with additional salt and sugar if desired. Serve warm or cold—or alongside schnitzel, which my husband requests every year for his birthday.

HACK IT

In a small pot, cook 1 cup peeled and chopped frozen or fresh butternut squash (4 ounces) and ¼ cup water until the squash is very soft (frozen chopped squash cooks the fastest)—10 to 40

minutes. Process the softened squash in a food processor or blender along with ½ cup store-bought applesauce and 1 tablespoon sugar (or 2 teaspoons honey), blending until smooth. Add another 1½ cups applesauce and pulse a couple of times until just combined. A 24-ounce jar of applesauce yields the perfect amount for this hack. After taste-testing this deliciousness, put the leftovers back in its original jar and keep in the fridge for up to a week.

SWAP IT

Want to use less sugar and get a little extra apple flavor? Replace the 1½ cups water with apple cider. Come fall we always have some in our house.

chewy granola bars

There are no veggies in this recipe, and even though I'm the Veggie Queen, I'm including this nonveggie gem because it's one that simply *needs* to be shared. It's incredibly easy, packed with lots of good stuff, and very well loved in my house.

One of the key "good stuff" ingredients is wheat germ, which I include in recipes whenever I can (check it out in my Banana Carrot Oatmeal Muffins on page 32 or my Chicken Parmesan on page 137). I like wheat germ because it's a simple, mostly flavorless way to seriously bump up the fiber, protein, and omega-3s in any dish. Wheat germ is the heart of the wheat kernel and the part of the wheat plant richest in vitamins and minerals—which, sadly, is normally stripped away to make flour. Combine this powerhouse with oats, nuts, and, of course, some sweet honey and creamy peanut butter, and you get a bar that's just as delicious as it is healthy. And no baking required!

MAKES 10 BARS

2 cups quick oats

½ cup **wheat germ**

½ cup chopped nuts, such as walnuts or almonds (see note)

½ cup dried cranberries

1 teaspoon ground cinnamon

¼ teaspoon kosher salt

⅔ cup honey

⅓ cup smooth peanut butter (see note)

¼ cup mini chocolate chips (optional)

1 Line an 8-inch square baking pan with parchment paper, allowing the paper to hang over the edges by 2 to 3 inches (this will allow you to easily lift the finished granola bars from the pan).

2 In a large bowl, combine the oats, wheat germ, nuts, cranberries, cinnamon, and salt, then set aside.

3 In a small saucepan over medium heat, cook the honey and peanut butter until they are fully combined and beginning to bubble—3 to 5 minutes. Pour this mixture over the oat mixture. Stir to coat the dry ingredients evenly and fully so that the entire mixture appears moistened; it will take a minute of stirring to ensure the honey mixture is evenly distributed.

4 Firmly press the oat mixture evenly into the pan to help the granola bars stay together (I like to use my hands and really press everything down, especially along the edges). Sprinkle the chocolate chips on top (if desired) and push them into the bars; don't push more than a couple of times, as the chocolate will melt slightly and you don't want to mush it around. Refrigerate the granola bars immediately and allow them to chill for at least 30 minutes.

5 After refrigerating, remove the granola bars from the pan using the edges of the parchment paper. Cut them into your desired size and enjoy! Once you have taste-tested,

store leftover bars in the refrigerator in an airtight container for up to a week.

SWAP IT

If you want to replace the wheat germ with something else, you can use ½ cup ground flaxseed, chia seeds, or hemp hearts, or simply ½ cup more oats.

NOTE

To make the bars nut-free, use a peanut butter alternative like Wowbutter and replace the nuts with ¼ cup more oats or ¼ cup ground flaxseed, chia seeds, hemp hearts, or shredded coconut. You can also sub the peanut butter for almond butter.

zucchini dill pickles

If you've never made pickles, you're missing out. It's really as easy as mixing sugar and vinegar, adding cucumbers, and in a couple of hours, magic! But why should cucumbers have all the fun? Zucchini make great pickles too, which makes sense since they are cousins of cucumbers, part of the same big family, bump elbows on holidays, and whatnot. However, unlike cucumbers, zucchini are slightly more tender, almost velvety (but still with a nice, crisp bite). And while canning pickles is fun, these pickles don't require those extra steps. They can live in the fridge for up to a month because of all that vinegar and sugar (natural preservatives!). Ha, not that they'll last that long!

— MAKES 1 QUART —

2 medium **zucchini**
 (1 pound), sliced into ⅛- to
 ¼-inch rounds or spears
Kosher salt
4 sprigs fresh dill or
 2 tablespoons roughly
 chopped fresh dill
 (optional; see notes)
1 cup apple cider vinegar
¼ cup sugar
3 whole garlic cloves
1½ teaspoons black
 peppercorns
1½ teaspoons yellow
 mustard seeds

1 Place the sliced zucchini in a colander set over a bowl or standing in your sink. Sprinkle the slices with 2 teaspoons salt, toss to combine, then set aside for 30 minutes.

2 Rinse the zucchini well, drain, and then transfer it to a 1-quart heat-safe glass jar along with the dill, if desired.

3 In a small saucepan, stir together the apple cider vinegar, ¾ cup water, sugar, garlic, 2 teaspoons salt, peppercorns, and mustard seeds. Bring this mixture to a boil over medium-high heat and cook, stirring occasionally, until the sugar and salt have completely dissolved—about 5 minutes.

4 Pour the hot vinegar mixture over the zucchini in the jar. Allow the liquid to cool, then cover the jar with the lid and chill the pickles completely in the refrigerator before serving—about 2 hours.

SERVING SUGGESTIONS

These pickles are my favorite additions to sandwiches or even white pizza, and I often serve them with my Eggplant Chicken Tenders (page 82) or my Homemade Hamburger Helper with Squash + Lentils (page 139). There is also not a happy hour that happens in this house without a cheese board complete with pickles, and maybe even a pickle martini. Cheers!

HACK IT

Just finished a jar of store-bought pickles? Don't throw away that liquid goodness! Follow Steps 1 and 2, but then add the zucchini directly to your old jar with the brining liquid. It will take a little longer for these to pickle since you're not heating the liquid, so leave them in the fridge overnight and enjoy the next day.

NOTES

* *These pickles are perfect refrigerator pickles, but are not good for canning, as the zucchini become very mushy.*
* *A wavy/crinkle-cut knife will get you wavy-shaped rounds.*
* *I've made these plenty of times with and without dill, and both versions are great. So if you've got no dill in the fridge, it does not mean no pickles!*

VEGGIES . . . FOR DESSERT!

I don't have dessert every day, so if I'm digging into something sweet, the last thing I want is a subpar healthy version that just leaves me disappointed. So let me be straight with you, these are not super healthy, low-cal versions of your favorite desserts. These are decadent, rich, mouthwatering desserts complete with sugar and butter because . . . desserts! BUT *there are also pounds of beets, cups upon cups of spinach, and chickpeas galore.* These are incredible recipes that are going to compete with your grandma's infamous peanut butter cookies, and they just might end up winning. Oh man, best to not tell her.

beets inside,
avocado on top

brooklyn blackout cake

Brooklyn blackout cake was invented in a German bakery in Brooklyn during World War II, having been inspired by blackouts that helped hide boats leaving New York's navy yard. Today, eating it brings back memories of "growing up" in NYC (where I moved when I was a fresh, green 18). It reminds me of more modern Brooklyn summer nights out with friends, days riding bikes along the river, and long, late conversations on little balconies. As a twist on the original, I'm adding beets to the batter, which intensify the rich, chocolate flavor and keep the cake moist. Complement this with avocado pudding and frosting, both made from one set of ingredients, and suddenly you are having your cake and eating it too—Brooklyn-style.

—— MAKES AN 8-INCH ROUND, TWO-LAYER CAKE (WITH 1 CUP PUDDING + 2½ CUPS FROSTING) ——

CHOCOLATE AVOCADO PUDDING FILLING + FROSTING

1 large **avocado** (10 ounces)

1 cup + 1½ cups powdered sugar, divided

⅔ cup unsweetened cocoa powder

½ cup maple syrup

1 cup unsalted butter (2 sticks), room temperature

Kosher salt

CHOCOLATE BEET BLACKOUT CAKE

3 small **beets** (8 ounces), roasted, or one 14.5-ounce can beets, drained well

3 large eggs

2 teaspoons vanilla extract

2¼ cups all-purpose flour

2 cups packed dark brown sugar

¾ cup unsweetened cocoa powder

1½ teaspoons baking soda

1½ teaspoons baking powder

½ teaspoon kosher salt

1 cup canola or avocado oil

TO MAKE THE PUDDING FILLING + FROSTING:

1 Cut the avocado in half, remove the pit, and use a soupspoon to scoop the flesh into the bowl of a food processor. Add 1 cup of the powdered sugar, the cocoa powder, and the maple syrup and blend until smooth, stopping to scrape down the sides of the bowl as needed. Add 2 tablespoons very hot water and blend again until the mixture is very smooth and creamy (this should give you about 1¾ cups pudding).

2 Scoop 1 cup of the pudding into a small bowl, cover it with plastic wrap, and refrigerate until it is completely chilled—about 30 minutes.

3 Meanwhile, transfer the remaining pudding to a large bowl, add the butter and a pinch of salt, then use an electric hand mixer (or stand mixer with paddle attachment) to blend the ingredients together until smooth. Add the remaining 1½ cups powdered sugar and blend again until smooth. Continue blending until the mixture is light and fluffy—2 to 3 minutes (this should give you about 2½ cups frosting).

CONTINUED . . .

treat stealer

... **CONTINUED**

TO MAKE THE CAKE:

1 Preheat the oven to 350°F. Spray two 8-inch cake pans with cooking oil spray, line with parchment paper, then spray the parchment paper with cooking oil spray as well (when cake sticks to the pan, it's the worst!); set aside.

2 Meanwhile, place the roasted beets, eggs, and vanilla in the bowl of a food processor or blender and blend until very smooth. In a large bowl, whisk together the flour, brown sugar, cocoa powder, baking soda, baking powder, and salt. Add the beet mixture and oil to the bowl with the flour mixture and stir until just combined, then stir in ½ cup boiling water until the mixture is smooth.

3 Divide the batter between the two prepared pans and bake, rotating the cakes once halfway through the baking time, until the cakes are puffed and a toothpick or knife

inserted into the center of the cakes comes out clean—35 to 40 minutes. Allow the cakes to cool for 20 minutes before removing them from the pans, then transfer them to a cooling rack to cool completely.

4 Once they are completely cool, trim the tops off the cakes so that they are mostly flat (this doesn't have to be perfect), reserving the trimmings. Place one cake cut-side-up on a large plate or cake stand, then spread the top of the cake with the chilled Chocolate Avocado Pudding Filling, leaving a ½-inch border without pudding around the edge. Press the second cake cut-side-down lightly on top of the pudding so that the pudding comes almost to the edges of the cakes. Refrigerate the cake for 1 hour to help the pudding and cake stick together and to prevent sliding when you cut into the cake later.

5 Meanwhile, finely crumble the cake trimmings and spread them out on a large plate or small baking sheet, allowing them to dry out slightly (you should have about 1 cup). Once chilled, remove the cake from the refrigerator and spread the Chocolate Avocado Frosting all over the top and sides of the cake. Sprinkle the dried-out cake trimmings on top, then slice the cake and serve.

SKIP THE PUDDING, GIVE ME MORE FROSTING!

To make an all-frosting, no-pudding cake or to make frosting for cupcakes, ignore the Chocolate Avocado Pudding + Frosting and make the following all-frosting version: In the bowl of a food processor, blend the flesh of ½ medium avocado, ⅓ cup unsweetened cocoa powder, ¼ cup maple syrup, and ⅛ teaspoon kosher salt until smooth, stopping and scraping down the sides of the bowl as needed. Add 1 tablespoon very hot water and blend again until the mixture is very smooth and creamy, then transfer it to a large bowl or the bowl of a stand mixer. Add 1 cup room-temperature unsalted butter (2 sticks) and use an electric hand mixer or a stand mixer to blend the ingredients together until they are smooth. Add 2 cups powdered sugar, blending again with the mixer until smooth, then continue blending until the mixture is light and fluffy—2 to 3 minutes more.

hacked veggie cupcakes

Boxed cake mix is one of my favorite shortcuts. It's inexpensive and includes cake flour (an ingredient most of us don't generally keep on hand). Add beans, spinach, zucchini, carrots, or beets to replace some of the water the boxes call for, and now you are truly onto something special. And the best part is the veggie versions taste *exactly* like the originals.

— MAKES 24 CUPCAKES —

vanilla or chocolate cupcakes with beans

One 15-ounce can **beans**, drained + rinsed (see note)
3 large eggs
⅓–½ cup canola oil*
1 box white, yellow or chocolate cake mix

Blend the beans, eggs, oil, and ½ cup water in a blender until very smooth, then transfer the mixture to a large bowl. Add the cake mix and stir until combined. If your batter is very thick, add a splash more water. Bake according to the package instructions.

NOTE *If you're making white or yellow cupcakes, be sure to use white beans like cannellini or navy beans. If you're making chocolate cupcakes, either white or black beans will work.*

vanilla or chocolate cupcakes with carrot

1 box white, yellow, or chocolate cake mix
1 cup **carrot juice**
3 large eggs
⅓–½ cup canola oil*

In a large bowl, combine the cake mix, carrot juice, eggs, and oil. If your batter is very thick, add a splash more water. Bake according to the package instructions.

NOTE *The color will be a slightly darker yellow if you are using yellow cake mix and a brighter yellow if you are using white cake mix. (The chocolate cupcakes' color is unaffected by the carrot juice.)*

vanilla or chocolate cupcakes with squash

2 medium **zucchini** or
  yellow squash (12 ounces)
3 large eggs
⅓–½ cup canola oil*
1 box white, yellow,
  or chocolate cake mix

Remove the ends of the squash, then peel and chop them (this should give you 2¼ cups chopped squash—10 ounces). Blend the squash, eggs, and oil in a blender until very smooth, then transfer the mixture to a large bowl. Add the cake mix and stir until combined. Bake according to the package instructions.

<u>NOTE</u> *You don't need to peel your zucchini or squash, but note that the skins do affect the color of white or yellow cake. You'll see green or yellow specks throughout the cupcakes.*

chocolate cupcakes with spinach

5 cups **baby spinach** (5 ounces)
3 large eggs
⅓–½ cup canola oil*
1 box chocolate cake mix

Blend the spinach, eggs, oil, and ½ cup water in a blender until very smooth, then transfer the mixture to a large bowl. Add the cake mix and stir until combined. Bake according to the package instructions.

pink or chocolate cupcakes with beets

1 medium **beet**, roasted and peeled
  (5 ounces), or one 8.25-ounce can
  sliced or whole **beets**, drained + rinsed
3 large eggs
⅓–½ cup canola oil*
1 box white or chocolate cake mix

Blend the beet(s), eggs, ½ cup water, and oil in a blender until very smooth, then transfer the mixture to a large bowl. Add the cake mix and stir until combined. Bake according to the package instructions.

<u>NOTE</u> *With white cake mix, the canned beets give you a light pink rose-like color, and the roasted fresh beet gives you a deeper pink/red color. Produce section precooked beets are not recommended, as the resulting color is more brown than pink.*

<u>GENERAL NOTES</u>
* *The recipes are based on popular brands of 15.25-ounce cake mixes that call for 1 to 1¼ cups water, ⅓ to ½ cup oil, and 3 eggs. Use the amount of oil the recipe on the box calls for.*
* *You can also use these recipes to make cakes.*

black bean brownies

One of my favorite features in this book is the Hack It note you'll find at the bottom of many of the recipes. I love to cook, but I also love a good shortcut. For this recipe, it's a toss-up as to which version I like best—the Hack It version calls for just beans, water, and brownie mix (no oil or egg), which makes it undeniably easy. But for the extra time spent on the from-scratch recipe, you end up with brownies that are extra gooey and chocolaty and truly irresistible. The good news is either version is going to give you all the fudgy brownie feels.

— MAKES 16 BROWNIES —

One 15-ounce can **black beans**, drained + rinsed

¾ cup packed brown sugar

½ cup unsweetened cocoa powder

⅓ cup refined coconut oil, melted (or ⅓ cup canola oil)

2 large eggs

2 teaspoons vanilla extract

¼ teaspoon kosher salt

¼ cup all-purpose flour

½ teaspoon baking powder

½ cup + ¼ cup semisweet chocolate chips, divided

1 Preheat the oven to 350°F. Position a rack in the center of the oven and spray a 9-inch square baking pan with cooking oil spray.

2 Puree the black beans, brown sugar, cocoa powder, coconut oil, eggs, vanilla, and salt in a food processor or blender until the mixture is very smooth. Transfer the mixture to a large bowl, add the flour and baking powder, and stir until the ingredients are just combined. Fold ½ cup of the chocolate chips into the batter.

3 Spoon the batter evenly into the prepared pan, smoothing out the top with your spoon if needed, then sprinkle with the remaining ¼ cup chocolate chips.

4 Bake, rotating the pan once halfway through the cooking time, until a toothpick inserted into the center of the pan comes out with only a few moist crumbs—15 to 25 minutes. You want to keep these fudgy, so a little underbaked is okay. Cool the brownies completely and then cut into 16 bars.

HACK IT

Process a 15-ounce can of drained + rinsed black beans along with the amount of water your brownie mix box calls for in a food processor or blender; transfer to a large bowl and stir together with the brownie mix until the mixture is just combined. There is no need for the oil, butter, or egg your mix may call for—beans, water, and the mix make incredible brownies all on their own.

black beans

pumpkin + oats

caramel pumpkin cake bars

What is a "cake bar," you ask? Well it's moist and slightly fluffy like cake, but more dense like a bar, if that makes sense (don't worry, it will). And while this richly flavored cake bar is totally capable of standing on its own, topping it with caramel and pretzels makes this a holiday-worthy dessert, the kind that goes on that fancy pedestal. Yep, it's that good.

— MAKES 16 BARS —

¾ cup quick oats
¾ cup all-purpose flour
½ teaspoon baking powder
½ teaspoon kosher salt
¾ cup pure **pumpkin** puree
¾ cup packed brown sugar
½ cup unsalted butter
   (1 stick), melted
1 large egg
1½ teaspoons vanilla extract
¼ cup + 2 tablespoons thick
   caramel sauce, divided
Sea salt or coarse kosher
   salt (optional)
16 mini pretzel twists, whole
   or crushed

1 Preheat the oven to 350°F. Spray a 9-inch square baking pan with cooking oil spray. Process the oats in a food processor or blender until they are finely ground, then transfer them to a medium bowl. Add the flour, baking powder, and kosher salt and whisk until combined; set aside.

2 In a large bowl, whisk the pumpkin puree, brown sugar, butter, egg, and vanilla until the mixture is fully combined and smooth. Stir in the oat mixture until all ingredients are combined, then spread everything evenly into the prepared baking pan.

3 Drizzle ¼ cup of the caramel sauce evenly on top of the batter in the baking dish, then bake until the cake bars are lightly puffed and a toothpick inserted into a spot where there is no caramel comes out clean—25 to 30 minutes.

4 Remove the cake bars from the oven and allow them to cool completely. Once the bars are cool, drizzle them with the remaining 2 tablespoons caramel sauce and sprinkle them with sea salt or coarse kosher salt (if desired). If you're using whole pretzels, arrange them on top of the caramel so that they form a 4 × 4 grid (4 across and 4 down); if you're using crushed pretzels, just sprinkle them on. To serve, cut into 16 squares.

NOTES

* If you're not serving the bars right away, wait to add the pretzels, as they will soften over time as they sit in the caramel sauce.
* To use up the leftover 1 cup canned pumpkin, make my Pumpkin Pie Granola (page 37) or simply freeze it for next time.

sweet potato cinnamon rolls

When I was a kid, my life basically revolved around cinnamon rolls—how to get money to buy them, how to convince my dad to make them, and whether, at my next birthday, I would stack cinnamon rolls into a cake or spell out my age with them.

As an adult, the love affair wavered only when I couldn't find anywhere to buy good cinnamon rolls and the versions I was trying to make at home ended up dry, lackluster, and tasting more like old dinner rolls. But it all changed when sweet potatoes entered the picture. Adding them to the cinnamon roll equation was the solution. It made my dough supple, slightly chewy, and delicate all at the same time. The end result is a sweet, gooey roll that would make my ten-year-old self very, very proud. The love affair is definitely back on!

—————— MAKES 12 CINNAMON ROLLS (WITH 1⅔ CUPS ICING) ——————

CINNAMON ROLLS

½ cup milk

1 teaspoon + ¼ cup packed dark brown sugar, divided

One ¼-ounce packet instant or active dry yeast (2¼ teaspoons)

1 medium **sweet potato** (8 ounces), cooked, peeled + mashed into ¾ cup puree (see note)

4 tablespoons unsalted butter, room temperature

1 large egg

2 teaspoons vanilla extract

2¾ cups all-purpose flour + more as needed

½ teaspoon kosher salt

1½ cups finely chopped pecans (5 ounces; optional)

⅓ cup heavy cream

SWEET POTATO FILLING

1 medium **sweet potato** (8 ounces), cooked, peeled + mashed into ¾ cup puree (see note)

⅔ cup packed dark brown sugar

6 tablespoons unsalted butter, room temperature

1½ tablespoons ground cinnamon

¼ teaspoon kosher salt

ICING

8 ounces cream cheese, room temperature

4 tablespoons unsalted butter, room temperature

1 cup powdered sugar

1½ teaspoons vanilla extract

¼ teaspoon ground cinnamon

TO MAKE THE CINNAMON ROLLS:

1 Heat the milk in a bowl in the microwave until it is just warm to the touch (105°F to 110°F). Stir 1 teaspoon of the brown sugar into the milk. Sprinkle the yeast over the top, then set the mixture aside until it becomes foamy—about 5 minutes. If it does not foam up, your milk may have been too hot or cold; try again (the yeast needs to be activated so that the rolls rise later).

2 In the bowl of a stand mixer fitted with a paddle attachment, mix the sweet potato, butter, remaining ¼ cup brown sugar, egg, and vanilla on low until all the ingredients are

CONTINUED . . .

combined. Add the yeast mixture and mix on low again; once the yeast mixture is incorporated, add the flour and salt and mix on low again until a thick and slightly sticky dough forms.

3 Once the dough comes together, replace the paddle attachment on the mixer with a dough hook and knead the dough on medium speed, adding up to ½ cup more flour if needed in order to make a smooth but slightly tacky ball that comes away from the sides of the bowl and sticks to the hook—3 to 4 minutes.

4 Transfer the dough from the mixing bowl to a lightly floured surface and form into a ball. Spray the recently used mixer bowl generously with cooking oil spray or drizzle lightly with olive oil. Place the dough inside and cover the bowl with plastic wrap or a kitchen towel and allow the dough to rise at room temperature until it has doubled in size—about 1½ hours. While the dough rises, make the Sweet Potato Filling and the Icing (see next page).

5 Grease a 13 × 9-inch baking dish with butter or spray with cooking oil spray. Once the dough has risen, punch it down, then turn it out onto a lightly floured surface. Knead the dough a few times until you have a nice ball, then roll it into an 18 × 12-inch rectangle about ¼ inch thick. Arrange the rectangle so that the longer side is parallel to the edge of the counter closest to you.

6 Spread the Sweet Potato Filling evenly over the surface of the dough, then sprinkle the pecans (if desired) over the top of the filling. Starting from the side closest to you (the longer side), tightly roll up the dough into a log. Cut the dough log crosswise into 12 equal slices, each about 1½ inches thick.

7 Arrange the rolls evenly in the prepared baking dish. Loosely cover the pan with plastic wrap or a kitchen towel, then allow the cinnamon rolls to rise at room temperature until they have doubled in size—about 30 minutes. This may take longer in a cool room. While the dough rises, preheat the oven to 375°F.

8 Once the rolls have risen, drizzle the cream over them. Bake the rolls until they are puffed and golden brown—25 to 30 minutes. Spread the Icing evenly over the tops of the cinnamon rolls and enjoy warm.

TO MAKE THE SWEET POTATO FILLING:

In a medium bowl, whisk the sweet potato, brown sugar, butter, cinnamon, and salt until the mixture is smooth (do this while the cinnamon roll dough rises—after Step 5), then set aside.

TO MAKE THE ICING:

In the bowl of your mixer, combine the cream cheese and butter on medium speed until they are well combined and smooth. Add the powdered sugar, vanilla, and cinnamon and continue to blend until the mixture is smooth and fluffy. You can also do this with an electric hand mixer. Refrigerate until you are ready to use.

NOTE

Cook the two sweet potatoes needed for this entire recipe by poking several holes in them with a fork. Microwave on high until very soft—5 to 7 minutes per potato (you can also cook in an oven at 350°F for 1 hour). Scoop the flesh out of the skin and mash until smooth (or use your food processor). This should give you 1½ cups puree; you'll need ¾ cup for the dough and ¾ cup for the filling.

SWAP IT

Instead of whole sweet potatoes, you can use canned sweet potato puree or canned pumpkin; a 15-ounce can will give you enough puree for the dough and filling.

MAKE IT AHEAD

I won't lie—these take a while to make, so to save some time on Sunday morning, make these the night before. Follow the recipe until the cinnamon rolls are cut and arranged in the baking dish (Step 8), but instead of allowing them to rise again in the pan, refrigerate them overnight (for a max of 12 hours). Remove them from the refrigerator in the morning and allow them to sit at room temperature for 1 hour, then continue with Step 9, adding the cream, baking as instructed, and finishing with the Icing.

white beans

chocolate chip cookies

Beans in your chocolate chip cookies? Yes! And not just because they pack loads of protein, but because they also provide great structure and moisture to this classic cookie. These cookies are *amazing*, but it wasn't easy to get here; this cutting-edge idea required endless batches of trial cookies as I figured out how beans and cookie dough could finally become friends. It was hard work—I ate a lot of cookies—but I took one for the team (you're welcome) and finally found the ultimate balance. The result is a soft, surprisingly airy cookie with a slightly gooey center. It is sure to become your family's favorite.

—————————— MAKES 24 COOKIES ——————————

¾ cup unsalted butter (1½ sticks)

¾ cup quick **oats**

One 15-ounce can **cannellini beans**, drained + rinsed

1¼ cups packed brown sugar

2 teaspoons vanilla extract

1 large egg

1 cup all-purpose flour

½ teaspoon baking soda

¾ teaspoon kosher salt

1½ cups semisweet chocolate chips or chunks (9 ounces) + more for a garnish

1 Heat the butter in a small pot over medium-high heat, stirring frequently until browned—about 5 minutes. You'll know it's ready because the butter closest to the pan will turn medium to deep brown and smell nutty. Once it does, be sure to remove the butter from the heat—it can quickly go from nutty, brown, and delicious to burnt.

2 Blend the oats in a blender until they are very finely ground and look like flour; add the cannellini beans, brown sugar, browned butter, and vanilla to the blender as well, and blend until all ingredients are very smooth and the mixture becomes slightly lighter in color. Add the egg and blend again until it is incorporated.

3 In a large bowl, stir together the flour, baking soda, and salt. Add the blender mixture and stir until combined. Add the chocolate chips (if you think your dough is warm enough to melt the chocolate, let it cool slightly first) and stir to incorporate. Refrigerate the cookie dough until it thickens slightly and becomes rollable—20 to 40 minutes. While the dough chills, preheat the oven to 400°F and spray two baking sheets with cooking oil spray.

4 Once the cookie dough is chilled, scoop out about 2 tablespoons, roll it into a ball, then place it on one of the baking sheets. Top the ball with a couple of chocolate chips, flattening the ball slightly (by about one-third) as you do so. Repeat with the remaining cookie dough. Bake

CONTINUED . . .

step 1   step 2   step 3

. . . CONTINUED

the cookies until they are golden brown around the edges and underneath—8 to 10 minutes. Transfer them to a cooling rack to cool completely. Once the cookies are cooled, enjoy or just eat them straight off the cookie sheet and burn the roof of your mouth like I do (#WorthIt)!

NOTE

Use any chocolate you like for this recipe; chopped dark chocolate and a dash of flaky sea salt on top never hurt anybody.

FREEZE IT

Freeze the cookies after baking and cooling; thaw at room temperature for 1 hour before eating.

SWAP IT

Replace the cannellini beans with other white beans like great northern beans, butter beans, or navy beans.

peanut butter cookies

You might not have known it, but peanut butter and beans were meant to be together. They make for a cookie with a moist, dense center that's not too cakey or crumbly, which is complemented by a sugar crust that's both chewy and crisp. Oh, and did I mention I'm nixing the egg and adding some of the liquid from your can of beans instead? Yep, it's called aquafaba, and it has all the emulsifying, binding, thickening, and rising properties of eggs. In this case, it actually works better than eggs, giving this cookie all the structure it needs without making it too fluffy (and it's free!).

— MAKES 32 COOKIES —

One 15-ounce can **chickpeas**

1½ cups smooth peanut butter (13 ounces; see note)

2 teaspoons vanilla extract

1½ cups packed brown sugar

¾ cup all-purpose flour + more as needed

⅓ cup granulated sugar, for topping

1 Preheat the oven to 350°F. Line two rimmed baking sheets with parchment paper. Drain the chickpeas, reserving ¼ cup of the liquid from the can (aquafaba coming at you!), rinse them, then add them to the bowl of a food processor. Process the chickpeas until they are very finely chopped, stopping a couple of times to scrape down the bowl.

2 Add the peanut butter, reserved aquafaba, and vanilla and blend until smooth; if the mixture is too thick for your food processor to handle, don't stress—just continue mixing by hand.

3 Transfer the mixture to a large bowl, add the brown sugar, and stir until the ingredients are well combined and smooth. Stir in the flour until well combined. The dough will be soft and oily, but you should be able to roll it into a ball; if you are unable to do so, add more flour, 2 tablespoons at a time, until you get there.

4 Place the granulated sugar in a small bowl. Using your hands, roll about 2 tablespoons of the dough into a

chickpeas

ball, roll it in the sugar, and place it on one of the prepared baking sheets. Repeat this process until all the dough has been used, placing the balls about 1 inch apart. Use a fork to lightly press down on each ball, flattening the cookies to about ½ inch thick and creating a crisscross pattern. If your fork sticks to the batter, dip it in water before creating the crisscross on each cookie.

5 Bake the cookies until they are mostly firm and lightly browned—17 to 22 minutes. Transfer them to a cooling rack to cool completely.

NOTE

Peanut butters that do not separate, like Jif or Skippy, work best here.

chocolate chip cookie dough ice cream sandwiches

Who doesn't love cookie dough? Of course, it's recommended that you don't eat it raw (did you know it's actually the flour more so than the egg that should only be eaten cooked?). That said, it's pretty irresistible, and I think many of us find ourselves sneaking a little taste (or a giant spoonful) whenever we're making cookies. But what if we made a safe-to-eat cookie dough complete with brown butter (and beans!) *and* stuffed it with ice cream? It's basically what cookie dough dreams are made of.

———— MAKES 12 SANDWICHES ————

¾ cup unsalted butter (1½ sticks)

1 cup all-purpose flour

¾ cup quick **oats**

One 15-ounce can **cannellini beans**, drained + rinsed

1 cup packed brown sugar

2 teaspoons vanilla extract

One 10-ounce bag mini semisweet chocolate chips (¾ cup + 1 cup, divided)

4 cups vanilla ice cream (2 pints)

2 tablespoons refined coconut oil

1 Heat the butter in a small pot over medium-high heat, stirring frequently until browned—about 5 minutes. You'll know it's ready because the butter closest to the pan will turn medium to deep brown and smell nutty. Once it does, be sure to remove the butter from the heat immediately—it can quickly go from nutty, brown, and delicious to burnt.

2 While the butter browns, heat the flour to reduce the risk of any foodborne illnesses associated with eating it raw or undercooked. Microwave it in a medium microwave-safe bowl for 30 seconds, stir, then return it to the microwave and cook until its temperature reaches 165°F—15 to 30 seconds more. Alternatively, bake the flour on a baking sheet lined with parchment paper at 350°F for 5 to 8 minutes. If the flour gets a little clumpy, that's okay. (Sometimes I heat a little extra flour, as occasionally some of it sticks to the bowl or baking sheet, leaving me with less for the recipe.)

3 Blend the oats in a blender until they are very finely ground and resemble the consistency of flour. Add the cannellini beans, flour, brown sugar, hot brown butter, and vanilla and blend until the mixture is very smooth; let the blender run for a minute to make sure the oats are really finely ground and everything comes together. Transfer the dough to a medium bowl, add ¾ cup of the chocolate chips,

CONTINUED...

. . . CONTINUED

and stir to combine (if you think your dough is warm enough to melt the chocolate, let it cool slightly first).

4 Line a 13 × 9-inch baking sheet or casserole dish with a large piece of parchment paper that goes up all the sides. Press the cookie dough evenly into the pan using your hands (it will be sticky, so spray your hands with cooking oil spray first). Freeze until the dough becomes firm—about 1 hour; you will know it's ready when you can lift up a corner of the cookie dough in one piece. When the dough is almost completely frozen, remove the ice cream from the freezer to soften slightly for the next step.

5 Once the cookie dough is firm, remove it from the freezer. Use the parchment paper to help lift it out of the baking sheet, and transfer it, with the parchment still on the bottom, to a cutting board. Cut the cookie dough in half widthwise, then place one half of it back into the pan, parchment-side-down. Spread the ice cream evenly over the top of the cookie dough. Place the second half of the cookie dough on top of the ice cream layer, parchment-side-

up, lightly pressing down on the ice cream without causing it to come out of the sides of the sandwich. Use a spatula or the back of a spoon to smooth out the ice cream around the sides of the sandwich, then return it to the freezer and freeze until it is completely firm—about 4 hours.

6 Once the ice cream and cookie dough are firm again, make the chocolate coating. Combine the remaining 1 cup chocolate chips and the coconut oil in a microwave-safe bowl. Microwave in 30-second intervals until the chocolate is fully melted, stirring every 30 seconds. Allow the mixture to cool slightly (it should be warm to the touch, but not hot), stirring occasionally so that it cools evenly.

7 While the melted chocolate cools, transfer the large ice cream sandwich from the freezer to a cutting board, removing the parchment paper. If desired, cut off the edges of the ice cream sandwich so that they are straight, then cut into 12 equal square pieces, wiping your knife clean after each cut. Transfer the ice cream sandwiches back to the pan, leaving some space between them.

8 Drizzle the tops of the ice cream sandwiches with the chocolate coating and return the ice cream sandwiches to the freezer. Freeze until the chocolate is set and the ice cream is firm again—about 30 minutes.

9 Remove from the freezer and fight the crowd of kids clamoring to get their ice cream sandwiches!

SWAP IT

* Instead of the chocolate drizzle, gently press the toppings of your choice into the ice cream on the sides of the sandwiches. Mini chocolate chips and chopped nuts work well, but avoid sprinkles since the color will bleed out into the ice cream.

* Quick oats work best here (don't use old-fashioned rolled oats), but you can also replace the oats with ¾ cup whole wheat flour or ¾ cup more all-purpose flour (totaling 1¾ cups flour).

chocolate spinach waffle sundaes

These guys are one of Ivy's favorite treats. When I was perfecting the recipe, she was not upset by the onslaught of chocolate waffles coming out of the kitchen. In the end, she agreed that we achieved the perfect amount of sweetness and crispiness for both an outrageous ice cream sundae and a fantastic breakfast treat. She ate two just to be extra sure.

─────── MAKES 2 TO 4 SUNDAES (WITH 8 WAFFLES) ───────

WAFFLES

5 cups **baby spinach**
(5 ounces)

1 cup whole milk + more as needed

2 large eggs

⅓ cup canola or avocado oil

2 teaspoons vanilla extract

1¾ cups all-purpose flour

½ cup unsweetened cocoa powder

½ cup granulated sugar

2 teaspoons baking powder

1 teaspoon baking soda

½ teaspoon kosher salt

½ cup milk chocolate chips

SUNDAES

Vanilla ice cream
Chocolate syrup

TO MAKE THE WAFFLES:

1 Preheat and grease a waffle maker on medium-high heat. Preheat the oven to 200°F to keep the waffles warm if needed.

2 Blend the spinach, milk, eggs, oil, and vanilla in a blender until the mixture is very smooth. In a large bowl, stir together the flour, cocoa powder, sugar, baking powder, baking soda, and salt. Then add the spinach-milk mixture from the blender and stir until just combined; if the batter is very thick, add a splash more milk. Add the chocolate chips and stir once more until they are incorporated.

3 Pour ⅓ to ½ cup of the batter into each compartment of the waffle maker, or whatever is appropriate for your machine. Cook the waffles until they are crisp and cooked through—4 to 5 minutes (you want to cook these on the longer side to get a nice crispy waffle that will stand up to the soft, creamy ice cream). Transfer the waffle to a cooling rack set over a baking sheet and keep it warm and crispy in the preheated oven until you are ready to serve. Repeat this process with the remainder of the batter.

TO MAKE THE SUNDAES:

Stack two to three waffles on top of one another. Scoop some vanilla ice cream on top and drizzle with chocolate syrup.

NOTES

* *Mini chocolate chips don't work well here, as they completely melt into the waffle as it cooks.*
* *Another pro tip—replacing the sugar with honey or maple syrup results in a soggy waffle, so as yummy as it sounds, steer clear.*
* *When eating these waffles without ice cream, I like them a touch sweeter, so I add ¼ cup more chocolate chips. The extra chocolate sometimes gets a little crunchy as it touches the waffle iron, so it may not look as perfect, but I like the occasional chewy + crunchy chocolate bite.*

PANCAKES

You can also make these into incredible fluffy chocolate pancakes. To make one 4-inch pancake, cook ⅓ cup of the batter in a pan over medium heat until bubbles start to pop on the surface and the pan side is slightly darker in color, then flip and cook until the other side is also darker and firm—about 3 minutes per side. Repeat with the remaining batter.

FREEZE IT

Waffles will stay good in the freezer for up to 5 months. Thaw from frozen by baking at 350°F for 10 minutes (waffles reheat best in the oven or toaster).

mint milkshakes with spinach

There are 5 cups of spinach—an entire package—in these two milkshakes! It's like having an extra-large salad *and* your dessert at the same time (except way more desserty and way less weird than that sounds). The spinach adds an extra boost of vibrant color while truly disappearing tastewise. It's such a simple and amazing way to get more veggies into your day, and also just outrageously tasty.

—————————————— MAKES 2 MILKSHAKES (ABOUT 4 CUPS) ——————————————

MILKSHAKE

5 cups **baby spinach**
  (5 ounces)
½ cup milk
4 cups mint chocolate chip
  ice cream (2 pints)

TOPPINGS

Whipped cream
Chocolate sauce
Crushed chocolate cookies
2 maraschino cherries

1 Blend the spinach and milk in a blender until the mixture is very smooth—you should basically have green milk. You will need to push down the spinach with your tamper (the stick thing that comes with the blender and fits in the hole on top of the lid). If you have lost your tamper like I have, scrape down the sides a couple of times and push the leaves toward the blades, then blend again.

2 Add the ice cream and blend until the mixture is smooth and the chocolate chunks are small enough to be sucked through a straw.

3 To serve, divide the milkshake between two large glasses. Top each with whipped cream, a drizzle of chocolate sauce, a sprinkle of crushed cookies, and 1 maraschino cherry.

NOTES

* If you want to make just one milkshake (half the recipe), you will not have enough liquid in the blender to puree the spinach into the milk (unless you have a small blender with a very narrow base). The best solution for a single serving is to make the full portion of the spinach-milk blend, then freeze half of that liquid (about ½ cup) for your next milkshake or put it in the fridge for another use (if using for something else, you can treat it like regular milk—use it in pancakes, French toast, or your next smoothie).

* Some brands of mint ice cream are very green and some are white; whatever color your ice cream is, this recipe works. The green mint ice cream looks about the same when blended with the spinach and the white mint ice cream turns a perfect minty-green color.

5 cups of spinach

chocolaty hazelnut hummus

Love chocolate? Love Nutella? Then you will love this!

Don't think of it as hummus (though basically it is)—think of it as a chocolaty dessert dip that will pair with anything and everything. Guaranteed! Well, not really guaranteed, this is a book, not an infomercial. Okay, good talk, enjoy!

—————————————— MAKES 1½ CUPS ——————————————

One 15-ounce can **chickpeas**, drained + rinsed

½ cup chocolate hazelnut spread, such as Nutella

2 tablespoons milk + more as needed

1 tablespoon unsweetened cocoa powder

1 teaspoon vanilla extract

½ teaspoon kosher salt

1 Bring a medium saucepan of water to a boil. Add the chickpeas and cook until they are very tender and mushy when pressed against the side of the pan with a fork—about 20 minutes (You can skip this step, but the more tender the chickpeas are, the creamier your hummus will be.)

2 Drain the chickpeas, then place them in the bowl of a food processor. The skins of the chickpeas will be broken down from boiling them, which will give you a smooth spread without having to go through the annoying process of peeling them before pureeing (but of course, if you peel them, your result will be even smoother). Add the chocolate hazelnut spread, milk, cocoa powder, vanilla, and the salt. Process this mixture until it is very smooth and creamy, letting the food processor run for at least 3 minutes. Add more milk if needed to get the consistency you want; start with an extra 2 tablespoons or even a touch more if needed.

3 To serve, transfer the hummus to a bowl and serve with your favorite dippers.

SERVING SUGGESTIONS

Serve the hummus alongside your favorite dippers, such as pretzels, apple slices, strawberries, or vanilla wafers. Or spread it on my White Bean Pancakes (page 25) and roll into logs, crepe-style. You can also drizzle it on my Sweet Potato Cinnamon Rolls (page 219) or slather it on my Chocolate Spinach Waffle Sundaes (page 232) for an extra-chocolaty bite.

s'mores pudding cups

S'mores have always been one of my favorite desserts. I'm definitely the person asking for "s'more" when it comes to that famous combo of marshmallows, chocolate, graham crackers, and now . . . *tofu*. Yes, tofu! Its silky texture mixes beautifully with the chocolate to create a rich and creamy, easy-to-make pudding. It's also easy to eat—irresistible, actually—with the addition of Marshmallow Fluff and crumbled graham crackers. And let's not forget all of that plant-based protein. S'more tofu, please!

— MAKES 6 PUDDING CUPS —

12 ounces milk chocolate chips (2 cups)

One 16-ounce package **silken tofu**

2 teaspoons vanilla extract

¼ teaspoon kosher salt

9 graham crackers (1 sleeve), crumbled (1½ cups) + more for garnish

One 7-ounce container Marshmallow Fluff (1¾ cups)

Mini marshmallows, for a garnish

1 Let's melt the chocolate! Roughly chop about 2 tablespoons of the chocolate chips, then set the chopped chips aside for a garnish. Microwave the remaining chocolate chips in a microwave-safe bowl in 15-second increments, stirring well after each time, until the chocolate is melted and smooth. Alternatively, you can melt the chocolate using the double boiler method: add 1 to 2 inches of water to a small pot and bring it to a simmer; place a large heat-safe bowl on top of the pot, making sure the bowl is held in place by the sides of the pot and the bottom of the bowl is not touching the simmering water (if it touches, remove some water); melt the chocolate inside the bowl, stirring frequently.

2 Carefully drain the tofu, then transfer it to the bowl of a blender. Add ¼ cup water, the vanilla, and the salt and blend until smooth. Add the melted chocolate and blend again until completely smooth (this should give you about 3 cups pudding). Refrigerate the pudding in a large covered bowl until it is completely chilled and thickened—at least 2 hours.

3 To assemble the pudding cups, layer ¼ cup of the pudding into each of six 8-ounce heat-safe glass jars (to make layering easier, you can also cut off the corner of a plastic food storage bag and spoon the pudding into it, creating a piping bag). Follow this with 1 heaping tablespoon of crumbled graham crackers in each jar, then 2 heaping tablespoons of Marshmallow Fluff, then repeat the layering once again with the same amount of pudding, graham crackers, and Fluff.

4 To serve, top the pudding cups with mini marshmallows, and use a kitchen torch to brown the marshmallows and the top layer of fluff if desired. Sprinkle the top layer with the reserved chopped chocolate. (If you want to get fancy—and I think you do!—prop a piece of chocolate upright on the side of each pudding cup.)

SWAP IT

You can replace the Marshmallow Fluff with whipped topping if desired; this will also make the pudding cup less sweet, which some prefer.

NOTE

Although silken tofu will give you the creamiest results (even without the best blender in the world), firm or even extra-firm tofu also works; you will need to blend more to get it as smooth as possible, adding up to ¼ cup more water if needed (so possibly ½ cup total).

chocolate avocado truffles

My son, Owen, led the charge in making avocados part of our regular rotation. He loves them so much that one of his first words was even "ah-oh"—maybe it was just a grunt of approval, but I swear he was saying "avocado." His big sister Ivy, however, will not go near avocados—which I guess is no surprise since she made it clear from her first taste of solid food—avocados!—that she preferred them on the floor rather than in her mouth.

My point in all this reminiscing is that avocados have played a big role in our house, and we always have them on hand. We also always have chocolate chips, and so if you're like us, you are already set up to have truffles tonight. The creamy, rich texture is unbelievable, and if you think for a minute that Ivy can resist avocado like this, you are very wrong. So simple—with a big payoff (hello, omega-3s, vitamins, and minerals)!

— MAKES 20 TRUFFLES —

1½ cups semisweet chocolate chips (9 ounces)
2 medium **avocados** (9 ounces)
1 tablespoon honey
1 teaspoon vanilla extract
¼ teaspoon kosher salt

TOPPING SUGGESTIONS

Unsweetened cocoa powder
Chopped nuts
Sprinkles
Coconut (toasted or untoasted)
Cinnamon sugar
Hot cocoa mix
Ground cookies

1 Microwave the chocolate chips in a microwave-safe bowl in 15-second increments, stirring well after each time, until melted and smooth. Alternatively, you can melt the chocolate using the double boiler method: add 1 to 2 inches of water to a small pot and bring it to a simmer; place a large heat-safe bowl on top of the pot, making sure the bowl is held in place by the sides of the pot and the bottom of the bowl is not touching the simmering water (if it touches, remove some water); melt the chocolate inside the bowl, stirring frequently.

2 Cut the avocados in half, remove the pits, and use a soupspoon to scoop the flesh into a food processor or blender. Add the honey, vanilla, and salt to the blender, then blend all the ingredients together until the mixture is mostly smooth, stopping and scraping down the sides of the machine as needed. Add the melted chocolate and blend again until completely smooth, then transfer the mixture to a bowl. Chill it in the refrigerator until stiff—at least 2 hours.

3 Once the mixture is stiff, add your desired toppings to small individual bowls and line a baking sheet with parchment paper. Use your hands to roll the chocolate mixture into

tablespoon-sized balls, then roll them each in a topping and transfer to the prepared baking sheet. Allow the truffles to chill in the refrigerator for 30 minutes before serving. Store leftovers in the fridge.

NOTE

A topping combo of cinnamon, chili powder, and unsweetened cocoa powder makes for truffles full of both sugar and spice.

AFTERWORD

willa's lemon bars

It's hard to write this book, talk about my children, share our lives with you, and not want to scream on every page: *Don't forget about my Willa!* For those of you who don't know, our first daughter, Willa, passed away in the womb on her due date. She was born sleeping on November 25, 2013, at 8 pounds, 4 ounces. That was also the day I was suddenly shot back into a world that expected us to be carrying a baby girl home in our arms. And, man, did those arms ache to hold her. But instead of sharing her smile, we shared our story and our pain, and it felt like that pain was never-ending.

In losing Willa, we lost our amazing, brown-haired, blue-eyed, big-handed little girl. We also lost the dream of starting our family. It had already been a long road to have Willa, and with her loss, the journey ahead seemed almost impossible.

But now, here I am, writing a whole book about my amazing children and the food we share. I truly didn't know if we would ever be here—the road didn't have bumps, it had mountains. And as grateful for our lives as I am, I cannot end this book without telling you that we are not a family of five, but a family of six. Having Willa was the biggest blessing of my life. She was the first to make me a mom. I got to keep her warm for nine months and even hold her hand for a brief time. Although you will not see her here in the pictures, laughing along with Ivy, running with Owen, or hugging Daisy, she is here, a part of our family, and she is a part of everything I do.

When pregnant with her, I craved nothing more than lemonade. If she were with us, I have a feeling she would love these lemon bars. So this recipe is for you, Willa. Love you, always and forever.

——————————— MAKES 24 BARS ———————————

OAT CRUST

1 cup old-fashioned rolled oats

½ cup granulated sugar

Zest of 1 lemon

¼ teaspoon kosher salt

1⅓ cups all-purpose flour

¾ cup unsalted butter (1½ sticks), melted

1½ teaspoons vanilla extract

LEMON FILLING

One 10-ounce bag frozen cubed **butternut squash** (about 2½ cups), thawed to room temperature

1½ cups granulated sugar

Juice of 4 large or 8 small lemons (¾ cup), room temperature

½ cup all-purpose flour

4 large eggs, room temperature

2 large egg yolks, room temperature

TO MAKE THE BASE:

1 Preheat the oven to 350°F. Line a 13 × 9-inch glass or ceramic baking dish with parchment paper, leaving some overhang to allow you to remove the bars easily (do not use a metal pan because it will give the bars a metallic taste, yuck). This is also a good time to let the squash, lemon juice, and eggs used for the filling come to room temperature.

CONTINUED . . .

2 Blend the oats, sugar, lemon zest, and salt in a blender until the mixture is very finely ground and has a flourlike texture. Add the flour to the blender and pulse a couple of times to mix the ingredients together (no need to clean out the blender after this step, as you will use it for the filling).

3 In a medium bowl, mix together the melted butter and vanilla, then add the oat-flour mixture and stir until a dough forms. Transfer the dough to the prepared baking dish and pat it down into an even layer (if you like, use the back of a measuring cup to press down on the dough to get it very flat). Prick the dough all over with a fork.

4 Bake the crust until it is lightly puffed and the edges are light golden brown—25 to 30 minutes. Remove the crust from the oven and allow it to cool for 20 minutes; this step is important because if you pour the lemon filling into a hot baking dish, the sides of the curd will cook too quickly and become rubbery. Reduce the oven temperature to 300°F.

TO MAKE THE FILLING + THE BARS:

1 While the crust is cooling, place the thawed squash in a fine-mesh sieve or kitchen towel and push/squeeze it well to remove as much excess liquid as possible; once most of the liquid is removed, you should have about ¾ cup squash. Transfer the squash to a blender along with the sugar and lemon juice and blend until completely smooth. Add the flour, whole eggs, and egg yolks and blend again until smooth. Use a spoon to remove any frothy bubbles that form at the top of the mixture.

2 Pour the filling from the blender onto the crust (it's okay if the crust is still a little warm, but the baking dish should be cool enough that you can touch it without oven mitts). Use a knife or skewer to pop any large air bubbles that form on the top.

3 Bake until the filling is fully set—about 35 minutes. Allow the bars to cool at room temperature for 1 hour, then transfer them to the refrigerator and cool completely (do not cover with plastic wrap, as it will cause condensation to form on the filling)—about 2 hours.

4 Use the parchment paper to lift the bars out of the baking dish and transfer them to a cutting board. Trim off the edges of the lemon bars using a large knife (eat these scraps— because you deserve them!). Top as desired; I like to use powdered sugar, candied lemons, and/or lemon peel.

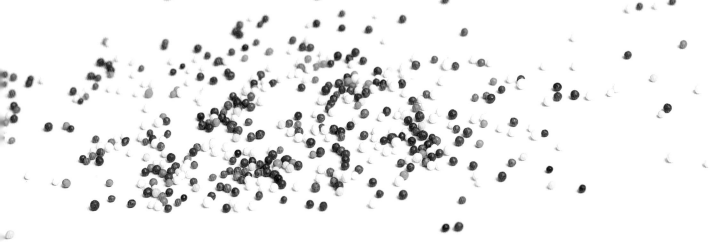

ACKNOWLEDGMENTS

EVAN: You have always believed in "Nikki Dinki Cooking"—believed in me. You are my forever partner, and I am so happy to be living this crazy life with you by my side. Thank you for supporting me, for supporting this book, and for always being the funniest guy I know.

CLAIRE SCHULZ: I am so happy I got to work on this book with you. You never once batted an eye at yet another crazy idea, instead giving me all the info and guidance I needed to make it happen—or not (which is sometimes the better choice). Your work is thoughtful and smart, and you never compromise on quality. I am very grateful for your guiding hand throughout this process.

TAMI ROOT FROCCHI: You made this book better, it's that simple. I could endlessly talk about your way with words, your attention to detail, and your creative soul. But for me it's your tireless commitment to making this book the best it can be that touched me the most. I almost equally love that you actually get what I'm saying when I talk about a ham and cheese wrap recipe getting too sexual (thanks for fixing that). You are such a unique and incredible person, and I'm honored to have you by my side. Thank you from the bottom of my heart.

ANDREANA BITSIS: I wrote a book I was insanely proud of, spending endless hours perfecting recipes. But all the while, I knew that if the dishes didn't *look* good, no one would actually make them. Well, *you* made them look good. You are a force to be reckoned with. Your photos brought the recipes to life and struck the perfect balance between sophistication and family fun. The unending effort and devotion you've put into this book matches the work I put into the recipes, and I am forever grateful for that. Thank you for committing to this labor of love in a way that made it reach its true potential. I will always think fondly of our mini Coca-Cola cheers on those endless shoot days.

TRACY CARTER: I am so lucky I got the opportunity to work with you. I am so grateful we connected and I got to experience just what a food styling genius you are. You are crazy talented, and I will always appreciate your willingness to muddle through the trenches with me and get it done—and get it done well! Your work shines on these pages.

MISS MISSY: I was always a fan of yours and I admire the way that you immediately engage anyone you talk to, even the smallest of us. I knew you could cook, but what I didn't know about was your attention to detail and your uncanny and innate sense of how to make things more streamlined, organized, and simply more beautiful. You were the missing piece in our photo shoot puzzle and I'm so grateful you were a part of this project.

ANTHONY MATTERO: With little else to go on but your gut, you made a choice to see just what we could do together, and here we are. You have always supported my ideas and helped me navigate this territory. I appreciate you and am thrilled to be on this journey with you.

STEFANIE BAUM, AKA "HAND": It's been such an honor to watch you grow as a chef and take on one new challenge after another. You are a badass, and I love your flair and passion. Thank you for continuing to help me test and retest this book, even during some very weird times. I will always appreciate your skills in the kitchen and, most importantly, your skills as a drunken hand puppet.

DAVE NICHOLAS: I love when we get to work together. I love the way you put my family and me at ease (Daisy eventually came around!). Thank you for your always-beautiful work; you are incredible at what you do, and I am blessed to be able to see my family through your lens.

GLENN YEFFETH: The first time we spoke, I knew there was potential for an amazing partnership. And after all is said and done, I see how on the money that initial feeling was. Your approach to publishing and creating books has allowed for all the incredible titles you perpetually crank out from under your umbrella. I am grateful you saw the potential of *More Veggies Please!* It's been, and will continue to be, a beautiful ride.

THE BENBELLA PRODUCTION, DESIGN + MARKETING TEAMS: Thank you for bringing my vision to life in the most beautiful, eye-catching, and streamlined way. I'm so grateful for your talents and dedication to this work. And as importantly, thank you for supporting this book in every way possible and making sure the *More Veggies Please!* word is heard!

DAMARIS PHILLIPS: It was around the 2,347th time I asked you for advice involving this book that I knew I had to include you in the acknowledgments. Thank you for your endless thoughts and creative ideas and for always lending an ear when I needed to talk something through. Your friendship is priceless.

PATRICIA BRIDGES OF BRIDGES POTTERY: I'm so thankful to have met you and to have your beautiful pottery shine on these pages. You have brought a bit of Long Island's finest artistry to this book.

BARBARA BRADY: What a joy it has been to get to know you and marvel at how effortlessly you make beautiful pictures happen, even when the scene is pure chaos. I'm so glad we were able to include some of your beautiful work on these pages.

MY RECIPE TESTERS: Where to start? I feel like we bonded on a level deeper than food—it was such an honor to share a very weird time in history with you. Besides that, your feedback and suggestions helped me perfect these recipes to a degree I've never experienced before. Because of you, I know they will work, for certain—for families just like yours. Thank you, from the bottom of my heart. And thank you for the encouragement, kind words, and cute kid pics along the way that motivated me during the hard times, assuring me that even when I didn't know it, I was on the right track.

From this group I owe an extra-special thanks to **AMANDA SEWARD, AMALIA BEARY GONZALEZ, GREGORY CABRAL, STEPHANIE HENNING, MELISSA BAKER, BECKY DIETRICH, DANA SUSMARAS, AND KELLY THOMPSON**. Your feedback was always extremely useful and deeply heard. We really got to know one another through this process, and I hope one day we can meet in person and share some great food. With extra veggies, of course!

RECIPE CHECKLIST

Made my Cheesy Green Eggs? Check it off! Prefer my Cauliflower Chive Risotto without the chives? Make a note of it! And don't forget to give your favorite recipes a perfect rating. And if you think you have what it takes to join my exclusive MVP! Club, all you have to do is make them all. As you cook, don't forget to tag me on Instagram **@NikkiDinki** and use the hashtag **#MoreVeggiesPlease** so I can see and share your creations!

breakfasts

Made it!	Recipe	Notes	My rating
☐	cauliflower + yogurt bagels	_____	☆☆☆☆☆
☐	avocado + pea toast	_____	☆☆☆☆☆
☐	cauliflower scrambled eggs	_____	☆☆☆☆☆
☐	cheesy green eggs	_____	☆☆☆☆☆

250

Made it!	Recipe	Notes	My rating
☐	white bean pancakes + waffles		☆☆☆☆☆
☐	zucchini french toast		☆☆☆☆☆
☐	cauliflower oatmeal		☆☆☆☆☆
☐	carrot apple oatmeal		☆☆☆☆☆
☐	banana carrot oatmeal muffins		☆☆☆☆☆
☐	strawberry cheesecake chia seed pudding		☆☆☆☆☆
☐	pumpkin pie granola		☆☆☆☆☆
☐	zucchini biscuits		☆☆☆☆☆
☐	carrot biscuits		☆☆☆☆☆
☐	vanilla yogurt coffee cake muffins		☆☆☆☆☆
☐	double chocolate chip muffins		☆☆☆☆☆
☐	lemon blueberry muffins		☆☆☆☆☆
☐	acorn squash bread		☆☆☆☆☆

lunches

Made it!	Recipe	Notes	My rating
☐	souped-up broccoli cheddar	_____	☆☆☆☆☆
☐	chicken noodle soup	_____	☆☆☆☆☆
☐	tomato soup with basil yogurt drizzle	_____	☆☆☆☆☆
☐	grilled cheese with sweet potato	_____	☆☆☆☆☆
☐	roasted garlic, spinach + tomato grilled cheese	_____	☆☆☆☆☆
☐	cauliflower egg salad sandwiches	_____	☆☆☆☆☆
☐	cauliflower crust lunch box pizzas	_____	☆☆☆☆☆
☐	chicken nuggets	_____	☆☆☆☆☆

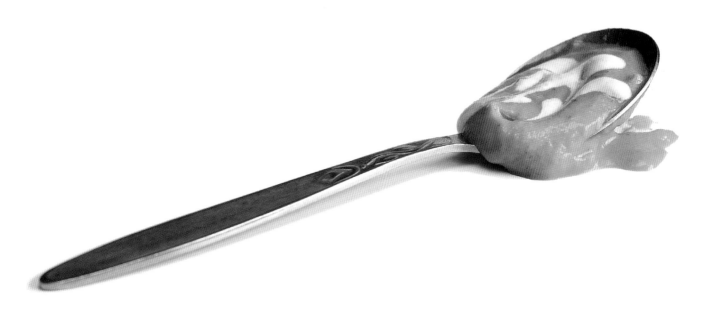

Made it!	Recipe	Notes	My rating
☐	raspberry beet vinaigrette		☆☆☆☆☆
☐	ham + cheese wraps in homemade spinach tortillas		☆☆☆☆☆
☐	eggplant chicken tenders		☆☆☆☆☆
☐	yellow squash corn tortillas		☆☆☆☆☆
☐	sweet potato tortillas		☆☆☆☆☆
☐	strawberry + chia jam		☆☆☆☆☆
☐	peanut butter + hummus spread		☆☆☆☆☆
☐	strawberry + beet jam		☆☆☆☆☆

dinners

Made it!	Recipe	Notes	My rating
☐	mac + cheese with cauliflower + sweet potato		☆☆☆☆☆
☐	taco meat with pinto beans		☆☆☆☆☆
☐	mushroom + beef bolognese		☆☆☆☆☆
☐	chicken cauliflower alfredo		☆☆☆☆☆
☐	spaghetti squash alfredo		☆☆☆☆☆
☐	cauliflower + potato gnocchi		☆☆☆☆☆
☐	eggplant marinara sauce		☆☆☆☆☆
☐	basil spinach pesto		☆☆☆☆☆

Made it!	Recipe	Notes	My rating
☐	penne alla vodka		☆☆☆☆☆
☐	pumpkin pasta dough		☆☆☆☆☆
☐	spinach pasta dough		☆☆☆☆☆
☐	eggplant parm meatballs		☆☆☆☆☆
☐	chicken pot pie with sweet potato crust		☆☆☆☆☆
☐	cauliflower chive risotto		☆☆☆☆☆
☐	chicken parmesan		☆☆☆☆☆
☐	homemade hamburger helper with squash + lentils		☆☆☆☆☆
☐	mushroom + onion burgers		☆☆☆☆☆
☐	ultimate veggie burgers		☆☆☆☆☆
☐	sweet potato pierogies		☆☆☆☆☆
☐	walnut + mushroom meatloaf		☆☆☆☆☆
☐	zucchini crust pizza		☆☆☆☆☆

sides and snacks

Made it!	Recipe	Notes	My rating
☐	creamed spinach garlic bread		☆☆☆☆☆
☐	butternut squash garlic rosemary focaccia		☆☆☆☆☆
☐	twice-baked potatoes		☆☆☆☆☆
☐	brown butter garlic mashed potatoes with cauliflower		☆☆☆☆☆
☐	garlic spinach naan		☆☆☆☆☆
☐	vegetable shapes		☆☆☆☆☆

Made it!	Recipe	Notes	My rating
☐	buffalo cauliflower wings		☆☆☆☆☆
☐	loaded queso		☆☆☆☆☆
☐	kale chips		☆☆☆☆☆
☐	garlic lime tortilla chips		☆☆☆☆☆
☐	pea guacamole		☆☆☆☆☆
☐	tofu ranch dressing		☆☆☆☆☆
☐	ranch pimento cheese spread		☆☆☆☆☆
☐	oat + cheddar cheese crackers		☆☆☆☆☆
☐	parmesan spinach crackers		☆☆☆☆☆
☐	buffalo party mix		☆☆☆☆☆
☐	butternut squash applesauce		☆☆☆☆☆
☐	chewy granola bars		☆☆☆☆☆
☐	zucchini dill pickles		☆☆☆☆☆

desserts

Made it!	Recipe	Notes	My rating
☐	brooklyn blackout cake		☆☆☆☆☆
☐	hacked veggie cupcakes		☆☆☆☆☆
☐	black bean brownies		☆☆☆☆☆
☐	caramel pumpkin cake bars		☆☆☆☆☆
☐	sweet potato cinnamon rolls		☆☆☆☆☆
☐	chocolate chip cookies		☆☆☆☆☆
☐	peanut butter cookies		☆☆☆☆☆
☐	chocolate chip cookie dough ice cream sandwiches		☆☆☆☆☆
☐	chocolate spinach waffle sundaes		☆☆☆☆☆
☐	mint milkshakes with spinach		☆☆☆☆☆
☐	chocolaty hazelnut hummus		☆☆☆☆☆
☐	s'mores pudding cups		☆☆☆☆☆

Made it!	Recipe	Notes	My rating
☐	chocolate avocado truffles	_____	☆☆☆☆☆
☐	willa's lemon bars	_____	☆☆☆☆☆

MORE VEGGIES PLEASE! MVP

☐ *I made them all!*

WHAT TO MAKE WITH WHAT YOU HAVE!

Got some zucchini sitting in the fridge? Or some extra carrot juice or chia seeds? Here's some inspiration for what to make with what you have on hand.

GOT AVOCADO? WHAT ABOUT . . .

Avocado + Pea Toast, page 20
Double Chocolate Chip Muffins, page 49
Pea Guacamole, page 189
Brooklyn Blackout Cake, page 209
Chocolate Avocado Truffles, page 240

GOT BEETS? WHAT ABOUT . . .

Raspberry Beet Vinaigrette, page 76
Strawberry + Beet Jam, page 92
Brooklyn Blackout Cake, page 209
Pink or Chocolate Cupcakes with Beets, page 213

GOT BLACK BEANS? WHAT ABOUT . . .

Loaded Queso, page 181
Vanilla or Chocolate Cupcakes with Beans, page 212
Black Bean Brownies, page 214

GOT BROCCOLI? WHAT ABOUT . . .

Souped-Up Broccoli Cheddar, page 60
As a topping for Spaghetti Squash Alfredo, page 105

GOT BUTTERNUT SQUASH? WHAT ABOUT . . .

Grilled Cheese with Sweet Potato (swap butternut squash for the sweet potato), page 66
Pumpkin Pasta Dough (swap butternut squash puree for the pumpkin), page 122
Homemade Hamburger Helper with Squash + Lentils, page 139
Butternut Squash Garlic Rosemary Focaccia, page 165
Loaded Queso, page 181
Butternut Squash Applesauce, page 200
Willa's Lemon Bars, page 243

GOT CANNELLINI (OR OTHER WHITE) BEANS? WHAT ABOUT . . .

White Bean Pancakes + Waffles, page 25
Vanilla Yogurt Coffee Cake Muffins, page 45
Tomato Soup with Basil Yogurt Drizzle, page 65
Chicken Nuggets, page 74
Chicken Pot Pie with Sweet Potato Crust, page 131

GOT LENTILS? WHAT ABOUT . . .

Homemade Hamburger Helper with Squash +
    Lentils, page 139
Ultimate Veggie Burgers, page 145

GOT MUSHROOMS? WHAT ABOUT . . .

Mushroom + Beef Bolognese, page 103
Mushroom + Onion Burgers, page 144
Ultimate Veggie Burgers, page 145
Walnut + Mushroom Meatloaf, page 152

GOT FROZEN PEAS? WHAT ABOUT . . .

Avocado + Pea Toast, page 20
Chicken Pot Pie with Sweet Potato Crust,
    page 131
Pea Guacamole, page 189

GOT PINTO BEANS? WHAT ABOUT . . .

Chicken Nuggets (swap pintos for the
    cannellinis), page 74
Taco Meat with Pinto Beans, page 100
Homemade Hamburger Helper with Squash +
    Lentils (swap pintos for the lentils), page 139
Ultimate Veggie Burgers (swap pintos for the
    lentils), page 145

GOT PUMPKIN PUREE?
WHAT ABOUT . . .

Pumpkin Pie Granola, page 37
Acorn Squash Bread (swap pumpkin puree for
    the acorn squash), page 55
Pumpkin Pasta Dough, page 122
Caramel Pumpkin Cake Bars, page 217
Sweet Potato Cinnamon Rolls (swap pumpkin
    puree for the sweet potato), page 219

GOT BABY SPINACH?
WHAT ABOUT . . .

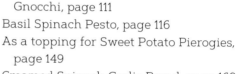

Cheesy Green Eggs,
    page 23
Double Chocolate Chip
    Muffins, page 49
Roasted Garlic,
    Spinach + Tomato
    Grilled Cheese, page 69
Ham + Cheese Wraps in
    Homemade Spinach
    Tortillas, page 79
As a topping for
    Cauliflower + Potato
    Gnocchi, page 111
Basil Spinach Pesto, page 116
As a topping for Sweet Potato Pierogies,
    page 149
Creamed Spinach Garlic Bread, page 162
Garlic Spinach Naan, page 173
Parmesan Spinach Crackers, page 196
Chocolate Cupcakes with Spinach, page 213
Chocolate Spinach Waffle Sundaes, page 232
Mint Milkshakes with Spinach, page 234

GOT FROZEN SPINACH?
WHAT ABOUT . . .

Banana Carrot Oatmeal Muffins (even more
    veggies variation), page 32
Spinach Pasta Dough, page 126
Vegetable Shapes, page 176

GOT SWEET POTATO? WHAT ABOUT . . .

Grilled Cheese with Sweet Potato, page 66
Sweet Potato Tortillas, page 88
Mac + Cheese with Cauliflower + Sweet Potato,
    page 97
Chicken Pot Pie with Sweet Potato Crust,
    page 131
Sweet Potato Pierogies, page 149
Sweet Potato Cinnamon Rolls, page 219

FREEZER-FRIENDLY RECIPES

As any parent knows, there's not always enough time in the day to whip up a meal from scratch. For those hectic days, which happen more and more often, I like to keep some of my kids' surefire favorite foods in the freezer so I can get their meal or snack on the table in a snap. Here is your go-to list of my favorite recipes that are just as good from frozen as they are fresh. Just take a look at the FREEZE IT note on each recipe for all the details.

breakfast

lunch

dinner

sides and snacks

dessert

FLAGGED RECIPES

top ten

Cheesy Green Eggs 23
Double Chocolate Chip Muffins 49
Sweet Potato Tortillas 88
Mac + Cheese with Cauliflower + Sweet Potato 97
Chicken Cauliflower Alfredo 105
Penne alla Vodka 119
Zucchini Crust Pizza 155
Sweet Potato Cinnamon Rolls 219
Chocolate Chip Cookies 223
Willa's Lemon Bars 243

classic

Cauliflower Scrambled Eggs 22
Cauliflower Oatmeal 30
Zucchini Biscuits 39
Grilled Cheese with Sweet Potato 66
Yellow Squash Corn Tortillas 85
Strawberry + Chia Jam 90
Chicken Cauliflower Alfredo 105
Pumpkin Pasta Dough 122
Mushroom + Onion Burgers 144

remix

Cheesy Green Eggs 23
Carrot Apple Oatmeal 31
Carrot Biscuits 43
Roasted Garlic, Spinach + Tomato Grilled Cheese 69
Sweet Potato Tortillas 88
Strawberry + Beet Jam 92
Spaghetti Squash Alfredo 108
Spinach Pasta Dough 126
Ultimate Veggie Burgers 145

INDEX

ABOUT THE AUTHOR

Cooking Channel and Food Network host, daytime TV regular, cookbook author, blogger, reformed picky eater, and mom of three, Nikki Dinki is changing the way families think about mealtime by using vegetables to enhance and balance everyone's favorite comfort foods. Appearing on the ninth season of *Food Network Star*, Nikki stole the spotlight with her unique vegetable-focused recipes and, among other accomplishments, went on to cohost Cooking Channel's *Junk Food Flip* and become a season regular on *The Wendy Williams Show*. Nikki's first cookbook, *Meat on the Side*, was released in 2016 and introduced the world to how special veggie-focused cooking can be.

Nikki currently lives in the NYC area with her husband, Evan; her twin three-year-olds, Owen and Daisy; and her five-year-old, Ivy. You can catch candid moments as well as exclusive recipes and mealtime tips and tricks, on Instagram **@NikkiDinki** or at **NikkiDinkiCooking.com**.

THE
END